THE
SECRET
IS OUT

When TERI MARTINI was a child, her father produced spy cards much like the baseball cards that are sold today. She collected the cards and became interested in the stories behind them. Her lifelong interest in espionage culminated in the writing of this book, her fourteenth for young readers. A former elementary and junior high school teacher, Ms. Martini is now an instructor for the Institute of Children's Literature. She lives in New Jersey.

LESLIE MORRILL has illustrated more than fifty books for children. He lives in Madison, Connecticut.

THE SECRET IS OUT
TRUE SPY STORIES

Teri Martini

Illustrated by Leslie Morrill

AN AVON CAMELOT BOOK

AVON BOOKS
A division of
The Hearst Corporation
1350 Avenue of the Americas
New York, New York 10019

Text copyright © 1990 by Teri Martini
Illustrations copyright © 1990 by Leslie Morrill
Published by arrangement with Little, Brown and Company, Inc.
Library of Congress Catalog Card Number: 89-27270
ISBN: 0-380-71465-5
RL: 6.1

The Little, Brown and Company editon contains the following Library of Congress Cataloging-in-Publication Data:

Martini, Teri.
 The secret is out : true spy stories / by Teri Martini ;
illustrated by Leslie Morrill.
  p.   cm.
 Includes bibliographical references.
 Summary: Highlights the daring escapades of such spies as Mata Hari, Lawrence of Arabia, Fritz Kolbe, Belle Boyd, and Kim Philby.
 1. Spies — Biography — Juvenile literature. 2. Espionage — History — Juvenile literature. [1. Spies. 2. Espionage.] I. Morrill, Leslie H., ill.
II. Title.
UB270.5.M37   1990   89-27270
327.1′2′0922 — dc20   CIP
[920]   AC

First Avon Camelot Printing: May 1992

CAMELOT TRADEMARK REG. U.S. PAT. OFF. AND IN OTHER COUNTRIES, MARCA REGISTRADA, HECHO EN U.S.A.

Printed in the U.S.A.

OPM   10 9 8 7 6 5 4 3 2

For Charles N. Martini,
with love and admiration

Contents

THE
SECRET
IS OUT

▪ INTRODUCTION ▪

Spies – Heroes or Villains?

Keeping a secret isn't easy, as anyone who has tried it knows. As long as there have been secrets, there have been people trying to uncover those secrets.

If you have ever peeked in someone's diary, snooped around for a hidden birthday present, or eavesdropped on a private conversation, then you have tried to obtain secret information. Perhaps you felt you had good reason to sneak around, but you probably knew that, if found out, your actions would not be appreciated by the person trying to keep the secret.

Suppose the tables were turned and you were the one with a secret. You would do anything to protect it, but that can be difficult. And sometimes it is hard to resist the urge to share a secret with a friend. Then you have to worry about whether or not that friend can be trusted to keep quiet. One mistake in judgment on your part could lead to your secret becoming public knowledge.

3

Spies make it their business to learn and trade secrets. They know how to locate and tap the best sources of private information without being detected. The term *spy,* or *secret agent*, may bring to mind a dashing figure, such as James Bond, in an exotic land. But in real life spies can turn up anywhere and they look and act like everyone else. Indeed, the most successful spies are those who seem the least suspicious, who inspire people to confide in them. They can make keeping a secret nearly impossible. Depending on your point of view, spies can be helpful or harmful.

The Bible tells the story of a man named Samson who lived thousands of years ago. His awesome strength was legendary; it was said that he once killed a thousand men with only the jawbone of an ass for a weapon. As long as Samson was there to protect his people, no one tried to harm them. But one group, the Philistines, wanted desperately to rule Samson's people, and they plotted against the powerful leader.

What, they wondered, was the secret of Samson's strength? The answer was the key to conquering him.

Samson had a beautiful friend named Delilah. One day she asked him something she had never asked before: "What makes you so strong, Samson? You can tell me. Friends tell each other everything."

At first Samson was reluctant to share his secret. But after a while he began to think there would not be any harm in it. Delilah was a friend, after all.

"My secret," he said, "is in my hair. If my hair were cut, I would lose all of my strength."

Delilah smiled and said nothing. That night, while Samson slept, she cut off all his long hair.

Unfortunately for Samson, Delilah was actually a Philistine spy, not a friend. And, just as he had told her, he was helpless without his hair. The Philistines were able to throw him into prison without a fight.

Are secret agents heroes or villains? The answer to that question depends mostly on whose side you are on. We may feel sorry for Samson, but to the Philistines, Delilah was unquestionably a hero.

We also have to take into account the spy's motives and the amount of risk involved. Delilah was aware that if she obtained Samson's secret, the Philistines were willing to pay her 1,100 pieces of silver for the information. We will never know whether it was money or loyalty to her people or some other motive that inspired Delilah to betray Samson. But we do know that she risked her life to do so.

The Boston silversmith Paul Revere, on the other hand, received no payment for risking his life to discover how and when the British troops would move against the Massachusetts colonists after the Boston Tea Party. When he learned the British planned to seize the guns and ammunition the colonists were hiding, Paul Revere rode all night, spreading the news. Captured once by British soldiers, he made a daring escape and continued his ride. Paul Revere was no richer after his exploits. He was a patriot, one of the Sons of Liberty. He believed the British were wrong to control the colonists, and he acted on his beliefs.

Because we know more about the reasons behind Paul Revere's famous ride than we do about Delilah's situation, it is a little easier to judge him a hero rather than a villain.

Paul Revere followed in the footsteps of many spies throughout history who in wartime learned the condition and movements of enemy troops. This kind of activity is known as military espionage. It was through such a spy that George Washington learned the best time to attack the enemy camped at Trenton during the Revolutionary War. This information resulted in the Americans' first great victory, on December 26, 1776.

Spies are useful in times of peace as well. They keep governments informed about what their own people or neighboring people are thinking and doing. Secret agents kept Elizabeth I of England one step ahead of those who wanted her throne. In Germany during World War II, the Gestapo let Adolf Hitler know who was an enemy and who was an ally. King Alfred the Great of Wessex did not have a reliable organization of secret agents, so he dressed up as a bard, or singing poet, himself in order to spy on his enemies in Denmark.

Secret agents can help individuals and private companies too. Anyone can hire a detective for a specific reason. Detectives, or private eyes, have used spying methods to locate lost dogs, stolen jewels, and missing persons. Because corporations compete with one another for customers, they want to be sure that no other company will come up with a better product. A company can hire a spy to nose out a competitor's secrets or to spy on employees suspected of stealing secrets. Employees of one company will sometimes sell secrets to another company about new products like cars, television sets, or laundry soap. Such activity is industrial espionage.

In the twentieth century, the profession of espionage has become more and more organized. *Intelligence* is the term now used to describe information discovered by spies. The first government intelligence agency paid for by public funds was formed by the British in 1909: the Secret Intelligence Service, or SIS. The Germans and the French soon formed similar agencies. The Russians formed the KGB. Since 1934, the FBI, or Federal Bureau of Investigation, has kept an eye on undercover activities going on inside the United States. In 1947, the United States organized the Central Intelligence Agency, or CIA, to gather information outside the United States.

Today, countries all over the world have intelligence organizations. Many, like the United States, have more than one kind of secret-service organization, with many departments within each of these. Governments even set up "counterintelligence" teams to discover and capture spies. As a result, secret agents are often spying on one another.

The work of a spy is difficult. He or she can spend weeks or months following false leads and then come to a dead end. Secret agents often spend a lot of time away from their families and friends. In addition to being lonely, it is a dangerous life: when they are caught, spies can be imprisoned or even killed.

Modern secret agents have new tools to help make their jobs easier. Instead of becoming involved in an enemy group, the spy can remain at a safe distance by using tiny electronic listening devices that can be planted in rooms or in telephones. In recent years, spy planes have been developed that can fly at high altitudes and photograph activities in other countries, thus gathering more information in a single day than the secret agent who travels from one place to another can over many weeks. Unmanned space satellites are spies in the sky that instantly send information to governments about what is happening in other countries without risk to any one spy.

The stories that follow are about real spies from history who did not have the luxury of today's technology. Their deeds were so daring that they became known throughout the world. Belle Boyd was only a teenager when she crossed a Civil War battlefield to carry a message through enemy lines. Captain Thomas Edward Lawrence, an Englishman dressed as an Arab, was able to move among enemy Turkish soldiers, speaking their language and learning their secrets. And in Hitler's Germany, Fritz Kolbe smiled and pretended to be a good Nazi while he stole important military secrets for the Americans.

The facts known about these spies may not be the whole story, however. Secret agents usually use code names and cover stories to confuse those who in turn

may be spying on them. Even after spies are captured, their "confessions" are often riddled with lies. It is precisely because secret agents are so good at dealing in secrets that some facts about them may remain forever buried.

Can we tell from what we know whether these spies were heroes or villains? You will have to decide for yourself. In any case, it is clear that, heroes or not, spies can have an important impact on the course of history.

▲1▲

The Gentleman Spy

When Captain John André found himself quartered in Philadelphia in the winter of 1778, he knew he had been right to buy himself a commission as an officer in the British army. Most of the patriots had fled when the British captured the city. The loyalists and neutrals who remained welcomed officers into their homes.

That winter in Philadelphia, the Revolutionary War seemed far away because the fighting had come to a halt during the cold weather. While members of George Washington's army huddled half-starved in rough camps on the opposite bank of the Schuylkill River, the people of Philadelphia indulged themselves with fine food, elegant dances, sleigh rides, and plays. Captain André was a gentleman who enjoyed such things. Wherever there were social gatherings, he could be found entertaining the ladies with his poetry and his ability to sketch portraits. Among the ladies who enjoyed this handsome young officer's company was seventeen-year-old Peggy Shippen.

But Captain André's life of leisure was short-lived. In the spring, news came that the French had agreed to support the Americans against the British. General William Howe and his troops were told to abandon Philadelphia and return to New York where they might have to face a French invasion.

Captain André was sorry to have to leave his friends in Philadelphia, but in New York he was pleased to receive an important promotion. He became Major André, aide to Sir Henry Clinton, the general in charge of His Majesty's forces in New York.

Not long afterward, Major André learned that Peggy Shippen had married the new American military commander in Philadelphia, General Benedict Arnold. Major André didn't hear from Peggy again for over a year. When he did, her mysterious message was delivered by a merchant from Philadelphia.

The message was a request for the major's help in obtaining from England some of the beautiful cloth and ribbons that Peggy liked to wear. But with Peggy's note was another letter, from a man who signed himself Monk. Major André realized at once that Monk was a cover name for Peggy's husband, General Benedict Arnold, who hinted that he was ready to give up the American cause and join the British forces.

André could hardly contain his excitement as he presented this news to General Clinton. If General

Arnold, one of the heroes of the battle of Saratoga, defected, many other Americans would follow and the tiresome war would be over.

But General Clinton was cautious.

"How do we know this letter is really from General Arnold?" he asked. "Why would such a brilliant officer want to give up his career and turn traitor?"

André knew Peggy well enough to know that she had expensive taste in clothes and that she loved to give lavish parties. There were rumors that General Arnold was pressed for money. He had used some of his personal money to pay his soldiers, and the Continental Congress had never reimbursed him. It was also said that he had used his military position to smuggle fine foods, wines, and clothes into Philadelphia for himself and his friends. The Philadelphia City Council could not ignore such behavior and was planning to investigate. Probably the worst insult of all was that Arnold had been passed over for promotions time and time again, even though Washington supported him as a brilliant soldier. Some said it was Arnold's arrogant behavior that kept the Congress from recognizing his worth as a military man. André knew an arrogant man would not stand for such treatment forever.

"I believe Arnold is fed up with the way the Continental Congress has treated him. He needs money, and for a price, he might well be ready to do anything," André said.

General Clinton was still not convinced.

"Find out what he wants, but proceed slowly," he ordered.

Messages were smuggled back and forth between André and Arnold for more than a year. Major André used the cover name of John Anderson. To keep his secret hidden, General Arnold repeatedly changed how he signed his letters, switching from Monk to Gustavus to Mr. Moore.

Finally, "Mr. Moore" had something so important to offer that General Clinton was ready to act. General Arnold had been made commander of West Point, the American fortress that protected the Hudson River and prevented British ships from traveling freely between New York and New England.

Capture of West Point and Arnold's defection to the British side would mean swift defeat for the Americans. Arnold agreed to sell all this for 500 British pounds. But first, he insisted, the British must send an agent to consult with him.

Major André was eager to be that agent. What better way could he serve his king and country than to be instrumental in ending the terrible war with the colonies?

General Clinton was at first reluctant to give him the assignment.

"It's too dangerous. You have no training in this kind of activity," he pointed out.

André argued that there was little he needed to know. All he was going to do was meet with General

Arnold at night on neutral ground and reassure him that the British planned to honor their end of the bargain.

"Besides, you could find no better agent. Arnold will trust me because his wife and I are friends."

Reluctantly, Clinton agreed that this was true, but before André left, Clinton gave him very specific orders that had to be obeyed: "Under no circumstances are you to go behind enemy lines. The agreement is to meet on neutral ground. Accept no papers and, above all, never remove your uniform for any kind of disguise. That way, should you be captured, you would be viewed as a prisoner of war and not a spy."

Major André saw very little danger in his assignment and he was anxious to begin his adventure. He sailed up the Hudson aboard the British ship *Vulture,* which anchored off Haverstraw Bay just inside British territory. The plan called for a rowboat to meet the ship under cover of darkness and take the major to the no-man's-land between British and American territory on the western bank.

All that night, André waited for a rowboat to appear. None came. For the first time, he felt uneasy. Perhaps General Clinton was right. The entire plot could be an American trick, but André hated to give up. He waited again and on the second night the rowboat arrived.

It was dangerous to be on the river even under cover of darkness, because the Americans shot at anything that moved in the water. But Major André made it safely to shore.

The first thing he noted about Arnold was that the general was twice Peggy's age, thirty-six or thirty-seven at least, and that he limped badly from his battle wounds. Together, the men moved deeper into the woods and talked. Dawn came, and to André's surprise, Arnold still felt their negotiations were incomplete.

"It will be impossible to reach the *Vulture* in daylight," Arnold told him. "You'd best come with me. My trusted friend Joshua Smith lives nearby. We can continue our talks over breakfast in his house and you can go back to the *Vulture* tonight." Arnold moved toward an aide who was holding two horses, expecting André to follow.

The young officer did not know how to respond. He looked back to the river, where the *Vulture* was riding at anchor, waiting for him, and remembered General Clinton's order: "Under no circumstances are you to go behind enemy lines."

But if he left now, the entire plot might fall apart. In seconds, he made up his mind. He followed the general to the large, white house above the river — behind enemy lines.

Over breakfast, the final plans were made. André was pleased with the way General Arnold had weakened the fort at West Point by sending a number of the soldiers away on other assignments. The iron chain that stretched across the Hudson to prevent British ships from sailing north had been taken up for repairs. Best of all, General Washington was expected to pay

a visit to the fortress. Why, the British could capture the fort and the commander in chief all at the same time! He was eager to get back to report the good news to Clinton. Even though André had disobeyed one order, the meeting had gone much better than he expected and he felt Clinton would approve of what he had done.

But just before Arnold left, he surprised André again by producing maps and detailed plans to help in the attack. He wanted the young officer to deliver them to his general. Faced with the prospect of disobeying a second command, André hesitated. He had been ordered to take no papers, but how could he insult General Arnold now, at the last moment? André made one feeble protest, gave up, and put the papers in his pocket. Surely, it would not matter if he held the papers for the few more hours he was to be behind enemy lines.

After Arnold left, their host, Joshua Smith, showed André to a room where he could rest. The long rays of September sun touched the waters of the Hudson with gold, and from the window, André could see the *Vulture* still riding at anchor in Haverstraw Bay. He prepared to wait for nightfall and even tried to sleep. With any luck, he would be on board the ship and safe within a few hours.

But luck was not running his way. Just before sunset, his host appeared again — this time carrying a broad-brimmed hat and a shabby jacket.

Major André stared at the clothes with distaste and

drew the folds of his dark blue cloak closer, covering the scarlet coat of his British uniform. He knew at once that something else had gone wrong. His throat went dry with fear.

It seemed the men who had rowed the major ashore the night before were unwilling to take the chance of rowing him back to the *Vulture*. Joshua Smith said he would have to go back a different way. It would mean riding farther north, to a spot where they could take a boat across the river to the eastern shore. From there, he said, he would guide "Mr. Anderson" to the nearest British outpost. Smith used the cover name carefully, as if he knew it was not André's real name, and as he offered the hat and coat, he eyed the dark cloak with a little too much interest. Obviously, Arnold had trusted Smith with a good deal of secret information.

But Major André could not worry about what Smith knew or did not know. His main objective was to get back to New York and give Arnold's plans to Clinton, even if it meant removing his uniform and donning a disguise. General Clinton had not foreseen all these difficulties. Surely, he would agree that the success of their plan was worth any risk, even this one.

When Smith left, André folded the papers Arnold had given him and placed them inside his stocking, making sure his boot covered them; then, unhappily, he took off his officer's jacket and, leaving it behind, slipped into the shabby coat and hat instead.

The sun had not yet set when Smith and André rode

to Stony Point, where they boarded a ferry that carried them to the east side of the Hudson River. Here there was an American fort, and Smith stopped to show the pass Arnold had given them. They were waved on through with no trouble. By then, it was dark, and the men rode several miles without meeting anyone. André relaxed a bit, until they were stopped by an American patrol. When the captain saw Arnold's pass, he helpfully suggested a place they could stay until morning.

"The roads to White Plains are dangerous," he said. "Robbers and ruffians lie in wait ready to attack unsuspecting travelers after dark. You'd be far safer traveling in daylight."

Another delay? André did not want to stop, but he could not convince Smith to ride on. They stayed at the farmhouse the soldier pointed out to them and André spent another uneasy night. He was up at dawn, insisting they leave at once.

Grumbling, Smith finally agreed, but he remained quiet and sullen as they resumed their journey. Off they rode into the rising sun, stopping only one more time, at a farmhouse, for breakfast. When they reached Pine's Bridge, Smith said this was as far as he was going.

"Your journey should be easy now because the territory beyond this point is neutral. Simply take the next turn to the left. From there, it's only a few miles to White Plains and the nearest British outpost," he said, handing André the pass he had been carrying for them.

With some relief, André bid Smith good-bye. At least now he was free to make his own decisions, and he could make better time by riding hard on this clear September morning. The country road was deserted and the woods on either side were alive with the brilliant scarlet- and gold-colored leaves of autumn. André hardly noticed as he pressed forward, anxious to reach a British outpost.

Afterward, Major André must have looked upon the next part of his journey with deep regret. If only he had not stopped for water, if only he had not taken advice from a young boy who told him to take the right fork in the road instead of the left, as Smith suggested, everything would have been different.

Confident that he was virtually safe now, Major André allowed himself to admire the fall foliage and consider how he might have sketched the scene if there had been time. When three rough-looking men sprang from the bushes, the major was startled, for the boy had told him the unfriendly Americans lurked on the other road. Major André recovered quickly. Smiling, he asked them what party they supported. When they replied, "The lower party," which is what the locals called the people who were sympathetic to the British, André thought he was home free.

"I'm a British officer," he said, and he asked them not to detain him, since they were all on the same side. But the men suddenly turned ugly, and he realized that he had fallen for a trick. They must be supporters of the Americans, he thought, and he produced

Arnold's pass. This did no good at all, because the only one of the three men who could read found it difficult to understand the writing.

André felt the cold breath of fear as he realized he had given himself away. He tried to think calmly. Perhaps all they wanted was to rob him.

André looked down the road. Could he possibly make a dash for it? Would his horse press through the three men who were blocking the road? Maybe not. In desperation, André offered the men his gold watch as well as the money Smith had left with him.

Still, the men were suspicious. They ordered him to dismount and to take off his clothing. Frightened now, André did as they asked, hoping against hope that they would be satisfied with his cloak and jacket.

But no! One of the men wanted his boots. André tried to distract the men with jokes, so no one would notice the bulky outline of the papers he had concealed in his stocking. The boots were quite a prize and the men fussed over them for a time. If the robbers would leave him now, the major felt, he could still reach a British outpost, even if he had to travel without boots. The men seemed to have lost interest in him and he was encouraged, but at the last moment one of them insisted on taking André's stockings too.

André's heart sank as the man snatched up the secret papers. The one fellow who could read a little made no sense of what they had found, but since the papers had been hidden, the men reasoned they were important and might be worth some money. The robbers took "Mr. Anderson" and his mysterious papers to Lieutenant Colonel John Jamison at the American outpost at North Castle, where he was arrested.

By September 24, Major André knew he had failed. He wrote to General Washington identifying himself so he would at least be treated as the officer and gentleman he was.

"The person in your possession is Major John André, Adjutant General to the British Army," he wrote.

He went on to explain the nature of his mission, leaving out nothing. The Americans, however, had already determined what kind of a plot was afoot and had moved to capture General Arnold. But they were too late. The general had escaped.

When General Clinton learned his aide had been captured, he wrote to the Americans, asking them to spare André's life. But the rules of war were clear. A spy caught in disguise behind enemy lines can expect nothing less than death. André knew the risks and was resigned to his fate.

On October 2, 1780, John André was hanged as a spy in Old Tappan, New Jersey, where a monument still stands, marking the spot. He met his death bravely, winning the respect of the American officers present, including Colonel Alexander Hamilton, who had come to know André while the British officer was in prison.

On the morning of his execution, André had his servant shave him as usual. When the servant felt such deep emotion that he burst into tears, André would have none of it and sent the man away until he could compose himself. The major showed no fear and shed no tears himself, but strode to his death with dignity.

Had André been successful in his mission, the course of history would certainly have been changed. The Americans would probably not have survived the double blow of losing West Point and their commander in chief, for it was Washington's noble spirit that inspired the army.

General Clinton must have forever regretted his decision to send an inexperienced spy to engage in secret negotiations with the enemy. By doing so, he lost a valiant soldier while ensuring an American victory. As for Benedict Arnold, he lived out his life in England after serving in the British army for a time, fighting against his own people. His name became a synonym for traitor. But John André will always be remembered for his valor and dignity as the gentleman spy who died for his country.

▲2▲

Abraham Lincoln's Personal Spy

Henry Davies was aware of every sound in the warm, pleasant room where he and his wealthy young friend Howard were visiting a woman. Davies had met Howard in the bar of the Fountain Hotel in Baltimore. Thinking Davies was a Southerner because of his soft New Orleans drawl, Howard had invited him out for the evening. Hours later, pretending to be drunk, Davies was sitting with his head bowed as if in sleep while Howard told his lady friend what he truly thought about Abraham Lincoln.

"I'd be willing to die myself to rid the country of this tyrant," he said, raising his voice. "You can be sure someone will do the deed and soon."

Davies grew very still. He tried not to breathe. This was the sort of information he needed.

"There's a man who is even now organizing a group of assassins," Howard was saying — not quite so loudly, but the words were clear enough.

25

His name, Davies thought. I need his name.

In seconds, he had it.

"Cypriano Ferrandini will succeed where others might fail," Howard said.

Davies had heard the name before. Ferrandini was a follower of the Italian assassin who had been executed for trying to kill Napoléon III.

Davies did not dare move or do anything that would reveal him as the spy he was. He had to wait until Howard was ready to leave. Only then could Davies slip away and report all he had learned to his chief.

Who was Henry Davies and why was he spying on this Southern gentleman?

In 1861, Baltimore, Maryland, was a busy place. The newly laid Philadelphia-Wilmington-Baltimore railroad brought many people to the city, including prominent figures who passed through Baltimore on their way to the nation's capital, only a few miles to the southwest. Soon, Abraham Lincoln would be traveling through for his inauguration in Washington.

At any other time, this event would have been a cause for celebration. Instead, Samuel Felton, the president of the Philadelphia-Wilmington-Baltimore Railroad, was worried. When Abraham Lincoln won the election, there were ominous rumblings from the Southern and border states. Many Southerners saw Lincoln as an enemy.

Rumors reached the North. Some said that Lincoln would never live to be inaugurated. Others said there was a Southern plan afoot to destroy the new railroad and cut the Northern states off from Washington, D.C. It was believed that angry Southerners had gathered in Baltimore to carry out these plans. Samuel Felton was not going to take any chances. He hired a private detective named Allan Pinkerton to protect his railroad.

Allan Pinkerton was not a native American. He was born in Glasgow, Scotland, and he came to the United States when he was twenty-three. He settled in Chicago, where he founded the first American detective agency. Eighteen years later, Pinkerton was the most famous detective in the United States.

In January 1861, Pinkerton arrived in Baltimore with a few trusted agents. Henry Davies, who had lived in New Orleans for several years and picked up the Southern drawl, was one of them.

Using the cover name of K. J. Allen, Pinkerton rented a house for himself and his men. They then went to work roaming the city, pretending to be Southern sympathizers who talked against Lincoln and the railroad. Finally, Henry Davies found Howard and overheard the information about the desperate men who were plotting to kill Lincoln.

Pinkerton put Davies's information together with what he and his other detectives had managed to learn and went to Philadelphia to warn Lincoln. The president-elect was traveling by train to Washington, stopping often to meet with his supporters along the way. Even after hearing about the conspiracy, Lincoln refused to cut his trip short lest he disappoint the people who were expecting to see him in Philadelphia and in Harrisburg, Pennsylvania. He did not take the threats of assassination seriously at all.

Perhaps a less dedicated man than Pinkerton would have given up. After all, he had been hired to protect the railroad, not to act as bodyguard for the president-elect. But Pinkerton was as stubborn as Lincoln and he was persuasive. He argued long and hard, carefully presenting the facts his investigation had uncovered.

"We have learned that even the police are disloyal, and should they be used as an escort, they would be of little help to you. I ask you to put yourself in my hands, sir."

Lincoln finally decided to heed Pinkerton's warning and agreed to do whatever the detective thought best.

Because Pinkerton's men had not been able to find out all the details of the plot, the detective had to guess where the attack on Lincoln would take place. In addition, he had to assume that there might be more than one group of assassins. Pinkerton concluded that the most likely place for an attack on Lincoln would be in Baltimore itself. Lincoln and his party planned to change trains there and would be going from one railroad terminal to another to continue the trip into Washington. The president-elect would travel across the city by carriage. Pinkerton thought the assassins might make their move during this trip through the city streets. It would be hard to protect Lincoln when the expected crowds of people came out to see him. Any one of the spectators could be carrying a knife or a gun.

"We must find a way to outsmart the assassins by changing Mr. Lincoln's travel arrangements," Pinkerton said.

On the night of February 22, 1861, Lincoln was scheduled to give a speech in Harrisburg. He had planned to begin his journey to Baltimore the next morning. Everyone was expecting Lincoln to arrive in that city on the twenty-third.

"We'll start twelve hours earlier," Pinkerton decided. "We'll need more men to check our route, trusted men. Not a word of this change in plans must leak out."

That night, Pinkerton was waiting with a special train to whisk Lincoln to Philadelphia after his speech in Harrisburg. In Philadelphia, another train would be ready for the special party. But this train had to be delayed with a cover story so no one would realize that Lincoln's party was coming aboard.

Pinkerton asked Felton, the president of the railroad, to send a message to the conductor of this train telling him to wait for a special package.

"The train must not leave without this package," the message said.

Before midnight, the package arrived — and so did the Lincoln party, who boarded the last two sleeping cars, which had been reserved by Detective Kate Warne, supposedly for a sick friend and his party. No one gave the travelers a second glance.

When everyone was settled, Pinkerton breathed a sigh of relief. The first part of his plan had worked well. Now his concern was the safety of the tracks.

The train would go straight through to Washington without stopping in Baltimore. But it was still possible that despite his precautions, news of the change in plans could have leaked out to Southern spies. When the train left Harrisburg, Pinkerton had the telegraph wires cut so no messages could be sent to the assassins in that way.

All that night, while Lincoln slept, the detective stood on the rear platform, puffing on his favorite cigars and watching for hooded lantern signals from his agents, who were stationed along the route. If he did not receive a signal that all was well, Pinkerton planned to stop the train and rush Lincoln to safety. The most dangerous places were bridges. The assassins could easily plant explosives and blow up a railroad bridge, destroying the train and killing everyone on it.

It was a long night for Pinkerton, with only the rhythmic clacking of the wheels on the track and the lonesome whistle from the engine to break the silence. But the train rolled through the quiet towns and cities without incident.

The next morning, Lincoln arrived safely in Washington, leaving the assassins in Baltimore astonished by his clever escape.

When news of the plot to kill Lincoln became public, the conspirators lost no time in running away. They did not learn until much later that Lincoln had ordered that none of them should be punished.

Lincoln was inaugurated president of the United

States on March 4, 1861. The Southerners had not succeeded in keeping him from taking office, but they refused to accept him as their president. The South set up its own government under President Jefferson Davis.

President Lincoln declared this act illegal under the Constitution, and he sent soldiers to force the Southerners to abide by the law. Still the Southerners refused and the Civil War began.

It is hard to imagine the history of the United States without the leadership of Abraham Lincoln. But if it had not been for Allan Pinkerton's investigations, his persistence and patriotism, Lincoln might have died in Baltimore before taking office. Instead, Lincoln survived to guide the North successfully through the Civil War and preserve the union of all the states. Four years later, however, long after Pinkerton had returned to Chicago, another group of conspirators, led by John Wilkes Booth, did succeed in assassinating President Lincoln.

Pinkerton and Davies were paid well for their services as spies for the railroad, but no amount of money can buy loyalty and integrity, the qualities that prompted Pinkerton and his agents to heroic action.

▲3▲

The Spy with "the Delicate Air"

On a dark May night in 1864, a ship slipped silently from its pier in Wilmington, North Carolina, and moved out to sea. This part of the Southern coast was carefully guarded by the Union navy, who were anxious to see that no ships left Southern ports to pick up guns and ammunition. The captain would be lucky to get his vessel, the *Greyhound*, past the blockade.

He wondered if his special passenger was frightened. Resting in a cabin below was the South's teen-aged heroine Belle Boyd, whom General Robert E. Lee himself had honored at Richmond for her bravery in serving the Confederacy.

After three years of spying, Belle had become so famous that she was recognized everywhere and it was impossible for her to go on with her secret mission any longer. She was being sent to London for her own safety, but she was also carrying secret letters from Jefferson Davis, president of the Confederate States of

33

America, to the British, whose help the South desperately needed if they were to win the Civil War.

Sleek and swift as the animal for which it was named, the *Greyhound* raced through the black waters. But sometime in the night, the captain realized he was being followed by a shadowy phantom. No matter how he tried to dodge and run, the Northern ship trailed him, moving relentlessly closer. At dawn, there was a brief battle and the captain was forced to surrender the *Greyhound* to a young lieutenant, Sam Wylde Hardinge, of the USS *Connecticut*.

Saddened by his failure, the *Greyhound*'s captain was certain Belle Boyd would never reach London now. But he had never been more wrong. Like so many military men before him, he had underestimated Belle's charm and courage.

Three years earlier, when Belle Boyd was seventeen, she was enjoying her first round of grown-up parties in Washington, D.C., and had no intention of becoming a spy.

Dozens of handsome young men were eager to be near Belle, to dance with her and to bask in the warmth of her friendly smile. Nothing a man said to her seemed unimportant as she gazed at him with her bright blue eyes. Belle's friends and relatives told her she was sure to marry a rich and handsome husband before the year was up.

Belle smiled and said nothing. She was not ready to

devote herself to just one young man, not yet. She was having too much fun.

There was talk at the parties of the bitter feelings between the Northern and Southern states, how they disagreed on states' rights, trade, and slavery. Talk like that often made Belle angry. She loved the Southern way of life, and she did not like to hear Northerners criticize her family and friends.

When the South seceded from the union of states and formed its own country, war broke out. Belle's father volunteered to fight for the South, and Belle and her mother returned to their home in Martinsburg, Virginia.

Belle was every bit as busy in Virginia as she had been in Washington. During the days, she worked in the hospital nursing wounded soldiers, but in the evenings there were parties and dances in Martinsburg too. Now, however, the men who came wore Confederate gray uniforms and proudly talked of fighting for the honor of the South. Belle dreamed of the valiant men who were fighting to protect her way of life.

It was not until that summer that Belle realized war is not all fine talk and dreams of adventure. In July, the Southern armies were being forced back by Northern soldiers. Martinsburg was captured and Belle's home was invaded by the enemy.

On the Fourth of July, Union soldiers celebrated their victory over the Southerners by drinking too much and singing loudly in the streets. The people of

Martinsburg locked their doors and hid behind heavily draped windows, but the Union soldiers broke in anyway. When men burst into Belle's house, her mother was there to meet them. The men tried to hang the Stars and Stripes over the door, but Mrs. Boyd said angrily, "Everyone in this house will die before they allow you to hang that flag here."

The men sneered and one of them pushed Mrs. Boyd roughly aside. Frightened and furious, Belle stepped from her hiding place behind the door with a gun in her hands. She pointed it at the Yankee intruder and ordered him to leave the house at once.

Perhaps he lunged at her. Perhaps he tried to take the gun away. Belle pulled the trigger and the Union soldier fell to his knees, blood staining his blue uniform.

Belle was still angry when the commanding officer questioned her about the shooting, but she hid it well. She knew how to handle men. She let her voice tremble as she described what happened. Then she stood with her head bowed, knowing very well how pretty she looked. If she simply held her tongue now, no real gentleman would blame her for what had happened.

The officer looked from the apparently helpless girl to the rowdy soldiers and came to a swift decision. He reprimanded his men and sent Belle home with guards to watch over her house so she and her mother would not be bothered again. Belle felt she had learned a valuable lesson. Perhaps there was a way she could help the war effort at home.

After that, Belle was not afraid to go anywhere in Martinsburg, whether the Union soldiers were there or not. The soldiers grew used to seeing the lively girl with the friendly smile and they enjoyed talking to her. Batting her long eyelashes, Belle asked the enemy soldiers what seemed to be innocent questions. Deliberately using the "delicate air" the soldiers so admired, she was able to collect valuable information that the Southern generals could use against the enemy. She wrote everything down and sent these secrets to General J. E. B. Stuart and to General Thomas "Stonewall" Jackson. Because she knew very little about how spies operated, Belle did not try to hide what she was doing by disguising her handwriting or using a code. Whenever she could find a messenger to carry her letters, she sent them off. Sometimes her maid or another servant was able to run through the woods, past the sentries, and over to the Confederate camps to deliver Belle's messages.

It was not long before one of the messengers was caught, though, and Union soldiers came to Belle's house to arrest the teenager. The officer who questioned her was very serious, so Belle was serious too. She listened intently as he told her what happened to spies captured in wartime, and then he sent her home.

Determined to do what she could for her country, Belle went right on sending messages — only now she tried to be more careful. For a while, one servant carried the messages hidden inside a large watch.

Several times, Belle herself rode behind enemy lines

to seek out Colonel Turner Ashby, a Southern officer who often disguised himself as a veterinarian and worked around Union camps picking up information for General Jackson. Colonel Ashby taught Belle to use a code. From then on, Belle thought of herself as a professional spy — and one day, a year later, General Jackson himself had occasion to thank her personally for her work.

It was May 1862. Belle had gone to visit relatives in the town of Front Royal, some miles south of Martinsburg. Belle's aunt owned a small hotel in Front Royal and there was usually plenty of room for visitors. But when she arrived, Belle found that the hotel was filled with Yankee soldiers and her aunt's family was living in a small cottage on the grounds. Belle was angry, but no one would have guessed her true feelings. She talked to the soldiers sweetly, as she always did.

Before long, these soldiers were telling her more secrets. Belle learned that there were not many Union men stationed in and around Front Royal, but that soon several other Northern armies would arrive, band together, and go after General Jackson. Jackson had only twenty thousand men, but he had been causing the Union army a good deal of trouble. Every time the Northern soldiers expected an attack, Jackson fooled them and popped up somewhere else. Once, General Jackson had nearly led his troops right into Washington, D.C. President Lincoln was set on having Jackson captured, and now the Northerners had a plan they thought would work. It would take a few days for three Union generals to assemble all their troops, but when they did, the armies would join forces and trap Jackson.

Belle was beside herself with anxiety. She knew General Jackson was nearby — less than a mile away, over the hills outside town. If Jackson attacked Front Royal now, he could surprise the Union troops before they were ready for him. If he waited, the other divisions of soldiers would overwhelm him by their sheer numbers. Somebody had to warn Jackson at once.

Belle did not even stop to change from her dress. She pulled a white sunbonnet over her light brown hair, ran out of the house, and headed for the back roads she knew so well from her childhood, when she used to go horseback riding with her cousins. She slipped past the Northern soldiers who were guarding the town and keeping an eye on Jackson's army.

For a time, she was able to hide among the trees and bushes, so the sentries did not even know she was there; but when she came to a meadow, there was nothing to do but make a dash for it. The Southern troops were just over the next hill.

The soldiers on both sides must have been astonished to see a girl racing between the lines. Some of the men were firing at each other, and shells burst around Belle, but still she ran. Suddenly, she saw a Confederate officer, Major Harry Douglas, riding to meet her.

"Belle, what are you doing here?" Major Douglas asked, hardly able to believe his eyes.

Breathless, Belle gave him the message for Jackson.

The grateful officer offered to escort Belle back to town, but she refused, saying she would make it back more quickly on her own.

"My love to all the dear boys," she said, waving her white bonnet.

General Jackson used Belle's information and attacked Front Royal that very day, winning a surprise victory against the Northern army and spoiling their plans to trap him.

On May 29, Jackson wrote Belle a personal letter, which she treasured for the rest of her life.

> *I thank you, for myself and for the Army, for the immense service that you have rendered your country today.*
>> *Hastily, I am your friend,*
>> *T. J. Jackson, C.S.A.*

The story of Belle's courage was told again and again. It was printed in newspapers and even reached the North. Belle became famous there and in Europe, too, where the French called her La Belle Rebelle.

The North could no longer tolerate such an effective spy, no matter how young she was. U.S. Secretary of War Edwin M. Stanton sent soldiers to arrest Belle and take her to the Old Capitol building in Washington, where a number of Confederate prisoners were being held. Belle's cell was not as bleak as the others in the prison filled with men. She had a room with a fireplace, but there were bars on her window and guards outside her door.

Belle refused to let her situation bother her. To keep her spirits up that first night, she sang her favorite Confederate song, "Maryland, My Maryland."

A hush came over the prison as her clear, sweet voice rose within its walls. Some prisoners later said they were moved to tears by her patriotism and courage.

Belle's time in prison was not pleasant, but she made the best of it. The guards were kind to her and by the time she was released, they were bringing her little gifts.

In August, Belle was sent home. Everywhere she went in the South, crowds cheered her. In Richmond, Belle sat beside General Robert E. Lee himself as soldiers saluted them. Belle accepted all this praise modestly, but in her heart she was proud of what she had been able to do for the South.

As soon as she reached home, Belle went right back to spying and carrying messages. She was arrested a second time. Altogether, she spent eleven months in Washington prisons, but she never lost her courage.

Belle knew the risk she was taking in carrying secret messages to London for the president of the Confederacy when she boarded the *Greyhound* in North

Carolina that May night in 1864. What she did not know was that she would fall in love with an officer of the enemy ship.

The moment Belle met Lieutenant Hardinge, she was fascinated by his appearance and gentlemanly manners. Hardinge was just as delighted with Belle. For her, he gave up his commission in the Union navy and joined the South. He helped Belle escape to England through Canada and a few months later Belle and Hardinge were married in London. There, Belle wrote a book about her adventures called *Belle Boyd in Camp and Prison*.

Belle Boyd voluntarily took personal risks for a cause she supported. No one guided her or paid her to gather military secrets. She did what she thought was right for the country she loved. Although Belle's efforts were not enough to change the outcome of the Civil War, the information she supplied helped the Confederate generals hold out a little longer and prolonged the conflict. Belle was one of the youngest spies ever to serve her country. Even those who disagreed with her motives had to admire her courage.

▲4▲

The Black Chamber

In 1905, Vienna, the capital of the Austro-Hungarian Empire, had one of the best counterintelligence agencies in all of Europe, thanks to the efforts of its chief, Colonel Alfred Redl. The work of such an agency is to discover and arrest enemy spies. Redl had introduced efficient modern methods of collecting and organizing fingerprints and it was not unusual for him to have hidden cameras behind pictures in his offices. After eight successful years as a counterspy, Redl was promoted to a position on the Austro-Hungarian general staff and transferred to another city.

Redl's successor was Maximilian Ronge, who wanted to live up to the colonel's reputation as a spy catcher. He continued the illegal practice of examining every piece of mail that went into or out of the city. Most Viennese citizens had no idea that mail was being censored, but in a room above the post office, a room known as the Black Chamber, Ronge's agents carried on their secret work.

On March 2, 1913, Ronge's spies discovered two envelopes containing large sums of money. There were no letters or messages with the money and the addresses were typewritten. What made the envelopes particularly suspicious were the postmarks. Both had been sent from a Russian border town. Altogether, the envelopes contained 14,000 Austrian kronen, a very large sum of money. Was it possible the Russians were paying off a spy in Vienna?

Chief Ronge was determined to find out. Sooner or later, the mysterious person would come to collect the envelopes addressed to Opera Ball, 13. Ronge ordered his department to keep two agents constantly on duty in a room near the post office. A special signal was arranged with the postal clerk to alert these agents the moment someone arrived and asked for the envelopes.

The agents waited through March, then April and most of May. Still no one came for the envelopes. On May 24, the two agents on duty were bored. One was half dozing and the other had left the room for a moment when the signal sounded. The men were slow to react, hardly able to believe that at last the waiting was over. By the time they reached the post office, they were too late: the clerk told them that a man in a well-cut tweed suit had already picked up the envelopes and had just left.

Hurrying into the street, the agents were just in time

to glimpse the man's cab driving away — but there was not another cab in sight to allow them to follow.

Neither of the agents wanted to report their failed mission to Chief Ronge. Fortunately, the first agent had had the presence of mind to memorize the taxi's number. They could question the driver and learn where the mysterious suspect had gone. No sooner had the thought come to mind than the agents looked up to see the very same taxi returning.

They motioned the driver to pick them up, and he took them to Café Kaiserhoff, where, he said, he had just dropped his passenger. The agents were relieved and thought it would be easy to identify the man if he was still at the café. Before getting out of the cab, one of the agents found another clue.

"Look! Here's a suede knife sheath on the seat. This could be his. Perhaps he used a pocketknife to open the envelopes."

Hoping to capture their man before he had a chance to get rid of the money or envelopes, the men took the sheath with them and hurried into the coffee shop. But they were disappointed. Not a single customer was sitting at any of the small tables that filled the room.

"No one has been in for over an hour," the owner told them.

Outside again, the frustrated agents looked up and down the street and spotted a taxi stand across the way. Perhaps their man had taken a second cab, hoping to throw anyone who might be following him off the trail.

One cab had just returned from taking a man who fit the suspect's description to the Hotel Klomser. The agents could hardly believe their good luck. They were closing in.

Trying to appear calm and unconcerned, the two agents strolled into the hotel. One of them looked around the lobby while the other spoke to the desk clerk. In the last hour, three guests had arrived by cab, he learned. The helpful clerk gave their names. One of them was Colonel Alfred Redl, the former intelligence chief, back in the city for a visit. Naturally, Colonel Redl was not under suspicion.

"Would you mind asking these men if any one of them lost this knife sheath?" the agent asked. "I found it in my cab just now and since it looks valuable, I thought the owner would be grateful to have it back."

The clerk agreed and the agents settled down to wait. Not long afterward, a man did come down to the desk and claimed the sheath.

It was Colonel Alfred Redl himself.

The agents were astonished and worried. Of course, there could be a very simple explanation for the colonel's receiving money from a Russian border town. In his work, the colonel had traveled all over Europe. Possibly someone was paying off a debt. Still, when it came to spies, you never knew who was with you and who was against you.

The matter had to be reported at once. While one of the agents made a phone call to the office, the other hurried after Colonel Redl, who led him down

several streets and disappeared into a building that had three exits. By this time, the second agent had caught up with the first and they were able to cover two of the exits. Once again, they were lucky. Redl was sighted hurrying away. He had quickened his pace, too. He obviously knew he was being followed. Suddenly, Redl stopped, drew some papers from his pocket, tore them up, and threw the pieces on the ground before rushing on.

This might be a trick, the agents reasoned. If they stopped to pick up the pieces of paper, Redl would get away. They ignored the papers and kept Redl in sight. Oddly enough, he simply returned to his hotel, where one of the agents waited while the other went back to pick up the papers.

When new agents arrived to relieve them, the first two went back to their office. There they were able to piece the papers together. And here was another clue. In his concern over being followed, Colonel Redl obviously had not been thinking clearly. Each of the papers was a receipt for mail, from three different cities — Warsaw, Lausanne, and Brussels. The addresses matched those found on a blacklist of enemy agents working in those cities.

Taking the receipt from the post office, Chief Ronge compared it to some personal notes Redl had given him before leaving his position. The handwriting was the same.

What was to be done now? With a heavy heart, Ronge contacted his superiors for advice.

Later that night, four government officials went to visit Redl, who offered no resistance. He admitted he had betrayed his country more than once.

"You will find all the information you want in the papers in my home," he said.

A less important man would have been arrested on the spot. But after a time, the officials left. One of them had carried a Browning revolver when he entered the colonel's room. He did not take it with him when he departed.

For a time, Colonel Redl's room was silent except for the scratching sound of his pen as he wrote letters to his brother and to a close friend. When he was through, Redl sat back and stared into space.

Once, he had been one of the most admired men in Austria. When his secret leaked out, as it surely would, he would be despised. While acting as chief of counter-intelligence, Redl had become a double agent who sold Austria's secrets to the Russians and identified his own agents in other countries so they could be captured and murdered. No one had guessed. No one would ever have known. If only he had followed his instincts and forgotten about the money waiting for him in the Vienna post office. Instead, he had risked one final contact and had been caught in a trap. He, of all people, should have known better.

The small desk lamp shone on the large Browning revolver. Finally, he picked it up and went to stand in front of his mirror.

At five o'clock the next morning, Redl's body was

discovered with a bullet through his head. On the table beside the two letters was a note, which read: "I die for my sins. Pray for me."

Redl's life as a double agent was over.

Chief Ronge soon discovered that Redl was a wealthy man, a millionaire many times over by our standards. There was more money in his bank accounts than he could have earned in a lifetime had he been an honest man. He owned two magnificent houses and four very expensive motorcars. There were cases of vintage champagnes in his wine cellars. The papers in Redl's Vienna home proved that he had been selling secrets not only to Russia but to other countries as well.

Colonel Alfred Redl was one of the most notorious double agents who ever lived. The extent of his treachery may never be known. To honorable men and women, there is no one more despised than an agent who betrays his own people for personal gain.

▲ 5 ▲

The Eye of the Morning

People from all over the world have flocked to Paris to enjoy the beauty of the city, its fine food, and its theaters. In 1905, a beautiful and mysterious dancer began performing in some of these theaters. She called herself Mata Hari, which meant "the Eye of the Morning."

Most people had no idea who Mata Hari really was or where she came from. Some said she was a princess from the island of Java in the South Pacific. Others thought she had once been a priestess in an Indian temple and had learned her dances there. Mata Hari did nothing to discourage these rumors, probably because the truth was so ordinary.

Mata Hari's real name was Margaretha Geertruida Zelle. She was born in 1876, in Holland, where she grew up and married an army officer, Captain Rudolph MacLeod. He took her to live on Java, one of the Dutch islands of the South Pacific. There, Greta, as her husband called her, had two children — a son, who died,

and a daughter. It was not a happy marriage and after eight years her husband deserted her.

When Greta was twenty-seven, she disappeared from Java, leaving her daughter behind. Not long afterward, the mysterious Mata Hari suddenly appeared in Paris. News of the dancer's grace and beauty traveled swiftly through Europe, and soon she had invitations to perform in Berlin, London, Madrid, and Rome.

Now successful and rich, Mata Hari was able to buy the expensive clothes, jewels, and furs she loved so much. Her friends were some of the most important people in European society, so she grew used to visiting in fine homes among wealthy people. Like them, she spoke several languages and was clever and charming.

For nine years, Mata Hari enjoyed the exciting life of a famous performer, but by 1914, when war broke out in Europe, her career was winding down. She was nearing forty. Younger dancers were more in demand and she was not asked to perform quite so often.

In the summer of 1916, Mata Hari met a young Russian officer, Vladimir de Masloff, and fell deeply in love with him. Since Russia was an ally of France, Masloff was able to visit Paris freely in spite of the war, which was in its second year. Soon, Mata Hari could think of nothing but marrying Masloff.

Unfortunately, Masloff was not a rich man. Early in the war, he was wounded in battle and lost the sight in his left eye. It was clear to Mata Hari that she would have to support both of them. Since her dancing career was nearly over, she knew she must find some other way to raise money. She decided to visit some of her wealthy friends. But when the famous dancer applied for permission to travel to Holland by way of Germany and Switzerland, she was surprised that the French were not willing to let her move about as freely as they had before the war.

Mata Hari considered herself a neutral and she argued for her rights. "After all, I am not French," she said. "I can have any friends that please me. The war should not be sufficient reason for me to stop traveling."

But the French were suspicious of anyone who wanted to visit Germany, France's enemy in the war. The war was not going well for the French that summer. Every time they launched an attack, the Germans seemed to know about it in advance. Munitions dumps were being blown up and ships torpedoed. The French were looking for enemy spies everywhere.

Mata Hari was questioned closely about the purpose of her trip by Captain Georges Ladoux, the chief of French counterintelligence.

During one of their conversations, Ladoux suddenly changed the nature of his questioning. He asked if Mata Hari had ever considered spying for France.

"What do you think such work is worth?" Ladoux asked.

Mata Hari did not know what to say at first, but she recognized an opportunity when she saw one. Perhaps spying for the French would be the perfect way for her to make a lot of money all at once.

"What is it worth?" she repeated. "A lot of nothing, I should think. I like to think big," she added, promising to consider Ladoux's suggestion.

When Mata Hari returned with her answer a few days later, she said she would agree to do such work for a million French francs. With that much money, she and Masloff could live happily ever after.

At first, Ladoux was shocked by her proposal. "A million francs is a large sum," he said.

"But you will see that I am worth it," Mata Hari told him.

Ladoux did not argue the point. Instead, he suggested that Mata Hari change her travel plans and go first to Spain, a neutral country, where she could contact Major Arnold Kalle, a German intelligence officer. If she could learn important information from Kalle, the French would consider paying her the money she wanted.

Mata Hari was pleased with the plan and confident that she could learn all the secrets the French wanted. But spying is a dangerous business and Mata Hari was an amateur.

What she did not know was that Ladoux had received a report from British intelligence identifying the famous dancer as a German agent. The French were testing her.

When Mata Hari reached Spain that December, she went to see the German officer, Major Kalle, even though she noticed two French agents following her everywhere she went. Perhaps the French were simply trying to protect her, she thought.

To gain the German's confidence, she had to give Kalle some information about the French, but Ladoux had given her no secrets. She improvised by telling the German intelligence officer gossip she had heard among her friends. The French had broken a German code, she told him. Morale in France was at a low ebb, she added, and there were severe shortages of food and supplies.

In turn, the major talked about German operations. Mata Hari fastened on two pieces of information. One had to do with the landing of German and Turkish officers by submarine in French Morocco, where they would certainly cause trouble. She did not learn exactly where they had landed or how many men were involved, which were facts the French would need to know. But Mata Hari was new at spying and was doing the best she could. She also learned that German spies carried crystals under their fingernails for making invisible ink so that they could send important messages to Berlin. When Mata Hari left Spain, Kalle gave her 3,500 pesetas.

Pleased with herself and sure now that she could be a successful spy, Mata Hari sent all she learned to Captain Ladoux. From their own spies, the Germans immediately learned what she had done and realized that she was acting as spy for France.

When Mata Hari returned to Paris in late December,

she tried to see Ladoux, expecting to be paid for her work so far and to receive a more important assignment.

Instead, on February 13, 1917, the French arrested her as a German spy.

The evidence against her was very strong. Ladoux's counterintelligence agents had picked up messages sent between Berlin and Kalle in Spain. They were written in the code the Germans knew the French had broken. From Berlin, they heard that Agent H21 should be given 3,000 francs but told that the results of her spying on the French were not satisfactory. A message from Kalle said that he had given H21 the sum of 3,500 pesetas and that she wanted a sum of money to be made available to her servants in Amsterdam because she had a lot of bills to pay there.

The French had no doubt that Agent H21 was Mata Hari.

No one was more surprised than Mata Hari to be caught in such a trap. She was innocent, she said, and for nine months she fought to convince the French that she had simply been trying to win Kalle's confidence by taking his money and feeding him gossip so he would share Geman secrets with her. Even the German information she had obtained did nothing for her. The French said they already knew about the landings in Morocco.

It took the French court only a few days in July of 1917 to convict the famous dancer of espionage. Although there were many espionage trials that year, none of them drew the crowds and the interest of the press the way Mata Hari's did. She was sentenced to die. For three months, Mata Hari was confined to her prison cell, waiting. In those days, it was the French custom not to notify the prisoner of the date of execution because the authorities felt it was kinder to announce the news at the last moment.

While she waited, Mata Hari wrote repeatedly to her powerful friends, but no one wrote back and offered to help her. Even Masloff, the man she loved, deserted her.

On October 15, in the hour before dawn, a dozen government officials marched down the corridor of Saint-Lazare Prison to the cell Mata Hari shared with two other prisoners. Awakening her, they delivered the terrible news. She was to be executed immediately. The waiting was over.

Resigned to her fate, Mata Hari dressed and prepared to leave for the grounds of the palace at Vincennes, where a firing squad awaited her.

Slowly, the caravan of black cars drove through the city streets, carrying the government officials and Mata Hari to the parade grounds, where witnesses had assembled. Dawn had not yet broken, and fog swirled along the streets and around the gates as they closed behind the dismal party.

Unassisted, Mata Hari walked boldly to her place in front of the firing squad. The chief of the military court

clerks walked onto the field and read his announce-
ment in a loud voice while the crowd of onlookers stood
hushed.

"In the name of the people of France, by order of
the Third War Council, [Margaretha Geertruida Zelle
is] unanimously condemned to death for espionage."

He walked off, leaving the prisoner alone at the
stake, her head held high as she gazed at the soldiers
who would carry out the sentence. When someone
approached to bind her hands behind her, she waved
him aside.

"That will not be necessary," she said. Neither
would she accept the blindfold.

The early morning sun glinted off the saber as the
commanding officer raised it, ready to give his men
the signal to fire.

Mata Hari smiled toward the nuns who had cared
for her in prison. She blew a kiss to the firing squad
just as the saber came down and the guns exploded.
Mata Hari crumpled to the ground.

No one who was present could help but be impressed by the courage Mata Hari had shown. What
was the secret of her great calm? Some people thought
it was the certain knowledge that she was innocent.
Others believed the rumor that Mata Hari never expected to die. Her powerful friends, they thought, had
told her that the guns of the firing squad would contain
only blanks. She would pretend to die. Later, she
would be taken to safety in another country.

But the guns did not contain blanks and Mata Hari's death was as dramatic as her life had been.

Afterward, many unconfirmed stories arose about Mata Hari. One of them suggested the Germans deliberately sent messages they knew the French would receive and decode to inspire them to execute their own agent. Hundreds of spies, including other women, were shot in France during World War I, but because Mata Hari was so famous, her story made headlines all over the world.

Mata Hari's career as a spy was brief and ineffective. The information she was able to bring to France, as well as the gossip she gave to the Germans, had no real impact on the war or the course of history, but the manner of her death was so courageous that it is not easily forgotten. Her fate was sad because it hardly seemed deserved. Mata Hari, a woman who loved adventure and felt no special loyalty to any country, played a dangerous game and lost. Whether she deserves the reputation or not, today her name brings to mind the vivid image of the mysterious and deadly female spy.

▲ 6 ▲

The Phantom of the Desert

The small band of Arabs came by night, riding their camels over the desert sands. With deadly purpose, the raiders moved through the dark toward their target: the steel tracks of the Hejaz Railroad, used by the hated Turks to transport trainloads of soldiers and weapons.

The white-robed leader, El-Aurens, planted explosives beneath the tracks. Speed was imperative. Already he could feel the vibrations of the oncoming train in the rails. El-Aurens uncoiled a cable, and carefully ran it from the explosives to a plunger that would allow him to set off the charges from several yards away.

Just as the train's engine reached the hidden explosives, El-Aurens pushed the plunger home. A violent explosion ripped through the desert night with terrifying force, sending the locomotive into the air and then down in pieces beside the ruined track. Fireballs soared into the black sky like flashes of lightning, revealing the white-robed leader. His men swarmed

forward to protect him, firing their rifles at any Turkish
soldier who had the presence of mind to fire a gun.
Seconds later, El-Aurens and his little band of raiders
vanished into the desert like phantoms.

El-Aurens was the name the Arabs had given their
leader, but the man beneath the gold-trimmed white
robes was known to his countrymen as Captain
Thomas Edward Lawrence of the British army, or
Lawrence of Arabia.

In 1916, England and France were at war with Germany. Turkey sided with the Germans. For years, the
Turks had controlled the Arabian lands. Countries like
Syria and Palestine had fallen before the fierce Turkish
warriors who pushed south and captured the Moslem
holy cities of Mecca and Medina.

When the Turks threatened to cross the Red Sea,
the British knew something had to be done to defend
Egypt, which was then a part of the British Empire.
The British did not want to weaken their forces in
Europe by pulling out soldiers to fight the Turks.
Somehow, another solution had to be found. A young
British intelligence officer came up with a workable
plan.

Twenty-eight-year-old Captain Thomas Edward
Lawrence was a rare Englishman with a perfect
knowledge of the Arab language. When Lawrence was
still in college at Oxford, he had gone to Syria alone,
against the advice of his professors, to study ancient
castles. He was told it was dangerous for a non-Arab

to travel among the Arabs because they were suspicious of foreigners. But Lawrence loved adventure. He went anyway and surprised everyone by making friends among the Syrians. He dressed like the Arabs, ate their food, and learned their language.

These Arabs were Bedouins — nomads who lived in tribes and followed their herds and flocks of camels, horses, and sheep. When food and water were exhausted in one place, they folded their tents and moved on to another. Lawrence learned of the Bedouin hatred for the Turks, who punished uprisings with cruel vengeance. If one Turkish soldier was killed, a hundred Arabs would be slaughtered.

What amazed Lawrence was that the Arabs refused to work together to drive the Turks from their land. The tribes were so suspicious of one another they could not unite to fight the common enemy.

After several months, Lawrence returned to Oxford, was graduated, and joined the army. In 1916, he was stationed in Egypt, just across the Red Sea from Arabia.

Lawrence had never lost interest in his Arab friends. When he learned that there had been a small but successful uprising in the Hejaz, the southern part of Arabia, Lawrence went to his superiors with his plan.

"Let me find out who has led the fight against the Turks. I might be able to persuade him to work with us to unite the other tribes against the enemy."

Lawrence received permission to visit King Hussein, the Bedouin ruler of the Hejaz. King Hussein had four sons — Ali, Abdullah, Faisal, and Zayd. Each son had a following of Arab warriors. It was Prince Faisal who had led the recent uprising and captured the holy city of Mecca, part of Medina, and several ports on the Red Sea.

Lawrence was impressed by the Arab prince's courage, but already the Turks had recaptured Medina and killed every man, woman, and child who was living there. It would not be long before the Arabs lost everything they had gained.

"You can't stop fighting now," Lawrence told the Arab leader. "You have to work together and come up with a plan to stop the Turks. The key to defeating them is to sabotage the Hejaz Railroad."

The Hejaz Railroad stretched for seven hundred miles from Damascus in the north to the city of Medina in the south. The Turks depended on their railroad to bring in fresh warriors and supplies. Cripple the railroad and the Turks would not be able to move their troops so easily.

Lawrence told the Arabs that the British were ready to supply them with guns and ammunition, as well as explosives. He promised that he personally would handle the explosives for them.

Prince Faisal immediately saw the wisdom of Lawrence's plan.

"With such explosives we can destroy their railroad entirely," he said.

"No, we don't want to do that," Lawrence explained. "We simply want to destroy parts of the railroad so that the Turks will have to continually use soldiers to repair it and guard it from attack. That way, the Turks will have fewer soldiers available to use in battle."

It did not take Lawrence long to convince the Arabs that his plan would work. There was something about this small man, not much taller than five feet, that suggested confidence and power.

Early in 1917, the raids on the railroad began. Each time Lawrence and his men blew up a bridge, destroyed a carload of soldiers, or derailed cars carrying food and ammunition, the Arabs won a victory, and they seldom lost one of their own men. As other Bedouin tribes saw how successful Captain Lawrence was, they became inspired to join the winning side under the brave British soldier.

The Arabs could not do enough for El-Aurens, the destroyer of trains. To show his appreciation, one prince gave Lawrence the splendid gold-trimmed white robes he always wore. Another provided him with the swiftest and best-trained camels to be had for racing across the desert sands.

Everywhere El-Aurens went, he was welcomed and praised by the Arabs. The Turks, on the other hand, feared him so much that they offered a monumental reward for anyone who captured this phantom of the desert.

In the fall of 1917, Lawrence learned that General Edmund H. Allenby, commander in chief of the British forces in Egypt, was ready to invade Palestine. General Allenby came to the desert to meet Lawrence and tell him what he needed to make this attack successful. From the city of Der'a, an important station on the Hejaz Railroad, there was a smaller track that branched off toward Galilee in the west. All Turkish troops and supplies passed through Der'a before moving into Palestine. If Lawrence's raiders could wreck part of that railroad, no supplies or new troops could be sent in to join the fight against the British.

During the first week of November, Lawrence left his camp with a few chosen men. It was eighty miles from the camp to the Yarmuk, a stream that flowed through the gorge beneath the railroad bridge. Lawrence reached the gorge in the early hours of the morning before daylight. He and his band had to leave their camels at the top of the gorge and climb down the steep slopes, carrying their explosives. In the darkness, it was hard to see how the bridge was guarded, but the saboteurs knew there must be a patrol.

They moved silently, with Lawrence in the lead. He had almost reached the pillars of the bridge where he meant to set his explosives when there was a dreadful clatter: one of the Arabs had dropped his gun. The silence was shattered by the clanking of metal hitting rocks as the weapon tumbled down the walls of the gorge to the water below. Instantly, the enemy guard rushed forward, shooting blindly in the direction of the sound. The Arab raiders scrambled for safety. With the guard alerted, it would be impossible to blow up the bridge. Disappointed, the men raced back to camp, stopping only long enough to blow up a train carrying four hundred Turkish soldiers on their way to Palestine.

The men were pleased with this small success, but Lawrence was very worried about having failed General Allenby, who was depending on him. He decided there was only one thing to do. He must capture the city of Der'a itself and shut down the entire railroad station. But before undertaking such a task, Lawrence needed information about how the town was fortified, how many soldiers were there, and where the guns were located. A spy would have to go into the city and gather this information.

Usually, Lawrence depended on a network of spies to keep him informed of troop movements and what trains to destroy. But there was no time now to send for the right spy and wait for his report. Lawrence decided to do the job himself.

"No!" his Arab friends protested. "What chance will a blond, blue-eyed man have of going unnoticed among so many dark-haired, dark-skinned Arabs?" they asked. "You'll stand out like a flag. You're sure to be captured and killed."

"Circassians are blond and blue-eyed," Lawrence argued. "I'll disguise myself as one of them."

Circassians were people from the north that the Turks had forced to join their army. Nothing anyone said could persuade Lawrence to give up the idea of spying himself.

"It's the fastest way to get what we need to know, and time is running out," he said.

Disguised in dirty, ragged clothing, El-Aurens and one Arab friend walked into Der'a the next morning. Slowly, they roamed the enemy city, noting the position of heavy guns and counting the number of soldiers present.

They had nearly all the information they needed except for the location of a secret back entrance to the city, something that could be valuable during a surprise invasion. Lawrence lingered, searching, alert for clues.

When a Turkish sergeant began following them, Lawrence took the precaution of giving his Arab companion orders: "If anything happens to me, get away. You must take the information back to camp."

When the Turkish soldier finally stopped Lawrence, he showed no fear, but stayed with his cover story.

"Why are you here?" the soldier demanded.

"I am just a visitor," Lawrence said. Obviously, he had not been recognized or the Turk would have made more of a fuss.

"Visitor? You're a Circassian deserter more likely!" the soldier accused. "You'll soon learn how deserters are treated," he said and took Lawrence away at gunpoint.

Helplessly, Lawrence's Arab friend looked on, knowing he must obey orders and escape.

That night, Lawrence was viciously beaten. Even through the horror of the ordeal, he realized he must not cry out in English or his captors would suspect who he really was. Finally, he lost consciousness and was left alone in a small, darkened room.

Just before dawn, Lawrence awoke and vaguely remembered a hoarse voice whispering to him in the night. Someone had told him that the door to the next room was unlocked. Had he dreamed this? Or had one of the guards felt sorry for him?

Painfully, he got to his feet and made it to the door. It opened easily. Taking time only to steal a tattered robe in the next room, Lawrence crept away and out into the city again.

Down dark alleys and around corners, he stumbled. Bleeding and hardly able to walk, he kept away from the main road, hiding in the shadows until, at last, he found himself outside the city. He fell to the ground, dizzy and weak, but triumphant. His mission had been successful after all. By accident, he had come upon the hidden passage out of Der'a.

As Lawrence made his way back to his camp, he promised himself that El-Aurens would be back and at that time the Turks would know who had come to Der'a. It took some weeks for Lawrence to recover from his wounds and by that time Allenby had taken Palestine, despite Lawrence's failure to cut off the railroad at Der'a.

But some months later, Allenby was ready to move into Syria and Damascus. Lawrence too was ready. His raiders took Der'a and in that city, where he had nearly lost his life on his spy mission, Lawrence set up an Arab government. He then hurried to Damascus as that city was taken by Arab and British troops and the Turks were driven from Arab territory once and for all.

His work completed, Captain T. E. Lawrence returned to England, leaving the Arabs forever grateful for all the Phantom of the Desert had done to help them regain their lands. Without this one courageous man, who knows how long the Arabs might have been subject to Turkish tyranny? Even the British themselves might have suffered serious setbacks in the Middle East during World War I. The legend of El-Aurens lives on in Arab countries; and among British intelligence officers, the success of Lawrence of Arabia has rarely been equaled.

▲7▲

The Spy without a Country

Captain P. W. Kenny of the British Secret Intelligence Service, the SIS, was surprised when Trebitsch Lincoln, a former member of Parliament, came to see him. Mr. Lincoln was not a native Englishman; he had made England his home by becoming a citizen. He was a short, stocky man who wore fine clothes. His thinning dark hair was parted in the middle and he had a mustache that added to his distinguised appearance. Lincoln spoke with a hint of a middle-European accent as he described the scheme he had in mind.

"I have a plan," he said, "that will assure victory and shorten the war. You will agree that without a strong navy to carry troops and supplies, the Germans are doomed to certain defeat."

In December of 1914, the English, French, and Russians — the Allies — had been at war for six months with the Central Powers, led by Germany. After being chased from the Mediterranean, the German battleships were hiding in their ports in the North Sea. The Germans had turned to using their U-boats, an early version of the submarine, to launch surprise attacks that resulted in the loss of several large British ships and many lives.

Captain Kenny was willing to listen to any workable plan to weaken the German navy and he asked Lincoln to go on.

"To destroy the German navy, you first must get their ships to leave their safe ports." Trebitsch Lincoln leaned forward in his chair. "We can trick them into doing that."

"How?" Kenny asked. The SIS had been exploring possible strategies for some time and had come up with nothing.

"I have a facility for languages and I speak German like a native," Lincoln said without a touch of modesty. "If I were to visit the German consul in a neutral country like the Netherlands, I could convince him that I am ready to betray England. I'll feed him information that you will give me concerning the whereabouts of a small fleet of British ships. Of course, you would have to be willing to lose those ships. After two such successful attacks, the Germans will trust me.

"Then I'll give them information about a much larger fleet, one that it would take the entire German navy to destroy. For such a prize, they will be willing to come out of hiding. But my information this time will be false. The British navy will be ready for a fight and the Germans will be overwhelmed and forced to surrender."

Trebitsch Lincoln sat back and waited for Captain Kenny to admire his scheme. Surely, such a daring plan was worth a vast sum of money — enough to pay off his creditors and get him out of the difficulties he now faced.

But Captain Kenny was a cautious man. He was not convinced that such a simple plan would fool the Germans. Besides, for such a scheme to work, Trebitsch Lincoln would need to know a good deal of secret information about the British navy. In the wrong hands, such information could prove fatal. How did Kenny know he could trust Lincoln? It was entirely possible that Lincoln was already in the employ of the Germans.

The captain decided to stall for time until he could find out more about the former member of Parliament. Kenny sent Lincoln to meet with the head of naval intelligence, while SIS agents investigated this overly confident, smooth-talking man. Their search led to Hungary.

Ignatz Trebitsch was only sixteen years old when his father announced that he had lost a great deal of money in the family business. Like his older brother, Ignatz would have to leave school immediately and go to work, something he did not enjoy. He much preferred spending his time in the coffeehouses of Budapest, not far from the small town on the

Danube where he was born. All afternoon and late into the night, Ignatz could be found entertaining his friends with stories of his travels to foreign cities. So convincing were his stories that no one guessed Ignatz was making them up on the spot. His friends bought him food and drink while encouraging him to tell still another story.

For a time, Ignatz enjoyed himself, but his family was growing impatient with him. Finally, he decided he would either have to get a job or run away.

Somewhere, he reasoned, he could find an opportunity that would make him rich. By stealing a gold watch and selling it, Ignatz got enough money to get away to the cities he longed to see.

He had not been away from home long when money became a problem again. In Hamburg, Germany, he came across a group of Irish Presbyterian missionaries who offered him food and lodging if he was willing to study their religion. Ignatz, who was Jewish, agreed to join them. On Christmas Day in 1898, he took on a new religion and a new name. He became a Presbyterian and was baptized Ignatius Timotheus Trebitsch.

He decided to continue his studies and become a minister. All the time he was studying, Ignatius did not have to work to earn a living. The Presbyterians took care of everything, and they were soon pleased to learn that Ignatius was a talented speaker. When he preached a sermon, everyone listened.

The Reverend Ignatius Trebitsch was sent to

Canada, where he learned to speak English and was successful as a missionary. He married a girl he had first met in Germany and started a family. But he was not content. He grew annoyed with his superiors for not promoting him quickly enough.

Three years later, in 1903, Trebitsch changed his religion a second time. He became an Anglican minister and moved to England with his wife and children. In the little village of Appledore, the Reverend Mr. Trebitsch was not as successful as he had been in Canada. The people did not seem to like his Hungarian accent. He was discouraged, but then the special opportunity that he had been waiting for all his life presented itself.

When his father-in-law died, Trebitsch's wife received a small inheritance. Trebitsch gave up the religious life, moved his family into a fine house, and changed his name again to something more English so that he could enter the business world. From then on, he called himself I. T. T. Lincoln because he was a great admirer of Abraham Lincoln, the former president of the United States.

Trebitsch Lincoln was not very successful at investing his money, but he met a wealthy man who gave him the kind of job he had always dreamed of having. Seebohm Rowntree was a sociologist, a person who studied society and how people got along with one another. Mr. Rowntree hired Lincoln to help him with his research.

In his work, Lincoln met important people in

governments all over Europe. It was not long before Lincoln thought he could be part of government too. He became a British citizen and was elected to Parliament on January 15, 1910, by just twenty-nine votes. But he had the support of important people. Winston Churchill, an influential member of Parliament, sent him a personal message wishing him success with the fine fight he was making for free trade, land reform, and popular government.

But in 1910, members of Parliament were not paid a salary. Lincoln's work for Rowntree was completed the year before, and although Lincoln had been paid very well, he was not careful with his money. His wife's small inheritance was also gone. He needed a way to make more money right away. Once again, he searched for that all-important opportunity and found it.

Lincoln decided to buy some Romanian oil wells. All the world depended on oil to run ships and other machines. It was only a matter of time before he would become so rich that he would never have to think about money again. He resigned from Parliament and borrowed money from Rowntree and various business acquaintances to buy the oil wells. All he had to do, Lincoln figured, was wait for the wells to produce the oil that would make him rich.

But Europe suddenly became unsettled. It was the summer of 1914. War broke out and people became worried about money. Those who had lent Lincoln funds wanted them back.

Lincoln did not have the money to give back. The

only thing he could do to calm his creditors was to have someone very wealthy guarantee that the debt would be paid if anything went wrong and the oil wells did not make money.

Lincoln carefully forged the wealthy Mr. Rowntree's name to just such a guarantee. If the oil wells paid off soon, Lincoln could buy back the guarantee and Rowntree need not know anything about the forgery. But time ran out and Lincoln had to sell his shares in the oil wells or risk going to jail for not paying his debts. Not long afterward, he once again forged Rowntree's name to keep himself out of trouble, but this time he was found out. By December of 1914, it looked as if he would be arrested at any moment.

Another man might have given up and left the country, but not Trebitsch Lincoln. He decided to go to Captain Kenny with his scheme. If he could pull off the plan, the British would be so grateful that no one would consider putting him in jail — and he would earn a good sum of money as well.

When the SIS did not give Lincoln a quick answer, he went to Rotterdam anyway and talked to the German consul general without the permission of the SIS, just to get things started. By the end of January, Lincoln was back in London, reporting to British intelligence about what he had already done.

Instead of thanking him, the British were angry and refused to have anything more to do with him. On February 16, 1915, a warrant was issued for his arrest on forgery charges, but by then Lincoln had left the country, just before his passport expired. He sailed to New York, and that spring a story entitled "Revelations of I. T. T. Lincoln, Former Member of Parliament, Who Became a German Spy" was published in a New York newspaper. The sensational story described how Lincoln had betrayed his adopted country and fled to the United States for refuge.

When the British heard about the story, they were horrified. Was this proof Lincoln was a German spy? If so, the British navy had had a narrow escape. But the SIS was not so sure Lincoln was telling the truth. They suspected he had written the sensational story for the money he could earn. They announced that he was a liar and a forger, and demanded he be arrested and returned to England immediately.

Lincoln was arrested in Brooklyn on August 4, 1915, but he would have to wait ten months to see if the American courts would agree to send him back. Perhaps they would not. After all, the Americans seemed to enjoy his colorful character.

Lincoln spent very little time in jail. During the day, he was allowed to go out to do research on the book he was writing about his adventures as a spy, and in the evenings he persuaded his police guards to accompany him to expensive restaurants. Several times, he escaped and turned up in New Jersey.

The British were so angry that the Americans could not seem to hold on to Lincoln that they hired the Pinkerton Detective Agency to find the prisoner. Finally, Lincoln was returned to England and spent three years in jail. When he was released, the British revoked his citizenship and sent him back to Hungary.

But it was not easy to dispose of Trebitsch Lincoln. On the boat from England to Rotterdam, Lincoln made friends with some Germans who were also being deported. Because he spoke German so well, the guards thought he was one of the Germans and he was easily able to get to Germany.

It was August 1919, and many political parties were struggling for power in Germany now that the war was over. One of the leaders was Wolfgang Kapp of the National Union. When Kapp met Lincoln, he was very impressed. Eight months later, when Kapp became the head of the German government, he named Trebitsch Lincoln press censor. Kapp's power lasted only a few weeks. Then, everyone concerned with the National Union had to leave Germany in a hurry or be arrested. When Lincoln escaped, he took with him important government papers, which he sold to Czechoslovakia.

When word of what he had done got out, Lincoln was not welcome anywhere in Europe. He moved from country to country, never quite succeeding at anything and often getting into trouble with the law. Stories followed him everywhere — tales about his willingness to act as a spy for any country that would pay him.

Finally, Trebitsch Lincoln disappeared from Europe.

In Tibet, there came to be known a Buddhist priest named Abbot Chao Kung. Despite his shaved head and long, flowing black robes, he bore a suspicious resemblance to Lincoln. Sure enough. The former minister had taken a new name and changed his religion once again.

For a time, he worked as a spy for Chinese warlords, but when it became clear that Germany and Japan were planning an alliance — one that eventually led to World War II — Lincoln began working for them instead. Colonel Joseph Meisinger, the agent of the Gestapo, or German secret police, in the Far East, sent a report to Berlin outlining Lincoln's proposal for propaganda radio broadcasting that would influence Tibet and India to join the German cause against England. It may have been a clever plan, but the Nazis did not trust Lincoln any more than the British had. He had to content himself with selling small secrets.

On October 6, 1943, Trebitsch Lincoln died of natural causes in Shanghai General Hospital. Lincoln had led an adventurous life, but his career as a spy, like his career as a businessman, was never successful. If the British Secret Intelligence Service had accepted his scheme to trick the Germans into bringing their navy out of hiding, perhaps Lincoln would have been proud to serve his adopted country with honor. On the other hand, he might have been tempted to aid the German government, especially if he saw an opportunity to make even more money as a double agent.

Judging from the way Lincoln moved from one career to another, the Allies were very lucky that the SIS never gave this spy without a country the chance to betray them. The man whose loyalty can be bought, as Trebitsch Lincoln's could, can hardly be considered a hero.

▲ 8 ▲

Mincemeat Swallowed Whole

Finding the right kind of corpse was difficult. Lieutenant Commander Ewen Montagu needed the body of a youngish man, one who had drowned or died of something that might suggest drowning. Montagu looked for several weeks before he heard about a fellow in his twenties who had died of pneumonia. What could be better?

A victim of pneumonia was likely to have water in his lungs, just like someone who had drowned. Delighted with his find, Montagu went off to inform his team of naval-intelligence officers.

During World War II, Montagu's job for British naval intelligence was to keep military operations secret and try to feed the Germans misinformation whenever possible. The body he found was part of a scheme he had dreamed up to confuse the enemy.

In the fall of 1942, the Allies were planning the invasion of Europe for the following summer. Since the Allied forces were gathered in North Africa after their victory over the Germans there, it would seem logical for the Allies to invade Europe through some point on the Mediterranean Sea. There were three obvious choices for an invasion point: the south of France, Greece, or Sicily.

When Sicily was chosen as the target, Montagu realized there was little chance of keeping this information a secret. In fact, he had learned from his network of spies that the Germans were aware of the Allied plans almost as soon as they were made.

The only possible solution was to try to convince the Germans that a landing in Sicily was only a cover story and that the real target was somewhere else. To do this, the British could send a spy with false information to the Germans. Or, they could send out a secret message about a new target and make sure the Germans were able to intercept and decode that message.

Both these methods were too obvious. Montagu was convinced the Germans would see right through them. He had another idea: Why not plant false information on the dead body of a Royal Marine and allow the Germans to find it?

But the members of his team were doubtful.

"You'll never get the Germans to believe the body was not a plant. They're too clever. And where would you get a dead body to use?" they asked.

Now Montagu had found a body, and it turned out that the young man had few relatives. When Montagu approached the father, all he asked was that his son's identity be kept secret and that he receive a decent burial.

With these matters decided, Montagu went to tell his men the good news. The team was pleased, but still cautious. It was fall and the plan was for the corpse to be discovered six months later, a few months before the invasion.

"A dead body will decompose by then," one of the men pointed out. "You won't get something like that past the Germans."

"We'll put the body in deep freeze," Montagu said. "Freezing will preserve it as it is now and make it appear as if the man had been dead only a few days."

When the counterintelligence team saw that Montagu had overcome most of the problems, they threw themselves wholeheartedly into creating the hoax. Not even their superior officers knew exactly what was going on.

Montagu made up cover stories for nearly everything they did. The fewer people who knew about the operation, the less chance there was of a leak.

To fool the Germans, it was vital that the phony British marine appear to be a real person. The first thing Montagu did was give the corpse a name so the team could talk about him as a friend. Major William Martin was the name Montagu chose, because it was such a common English name. There were several Royal Marines named Martin. Later, when the story came out, other officers would not be surprised to hear that name and might even suspect they knew this Major Martin.

The team decided that Major Martin would be on a special assignment, carrying secret papers to British officers in North Africa. The papers would reveal the top-secret information that Sicily was not the invasion point at all — it was Greece!

Poor Major Martin would have an accident at sea and his body would be found drifting toward Huelva, a fishing village off the coast of Spain. Spain was chosen because it was a neutral country. Both British and German officials were present there. Montagu hoped that a certain German spy he knew of in Huelva would make it his business to learn about the secret papers the Major was carrying.

Naturally, the official letters would be carried in a locked black briefcase, the kind used by most couriers. In his pockets, Major Martin would be carrying personal papers and effects that would tell something about him and convince the Germans that this was a real man and not a hoax. The important thing was to get the Germans to swallow the story whole. So Montagu decided to call their operation "Mincemeat."

To begin with, Major Martin needed identity papers with a photograph. After several tries, the team found it impossible to photograph the dead man without coming up with a picture that looked like what it was — the picture of a corpse. By a stroke of good luck, Montagu came upon a man who resembled the corpse strongly. The man agreed to dress up as a Royal Marine and be photographed without knowing the reason why, except that it had to do with a counterspy operation.

Then the team considered what sort of man Major Martin was and what they could plant on his body to suggest that he was a real person with family and friends. They decided that Major Martin had recently become engaged and might well be carrying around some love letters and a picture of his girl.

Montagu told the women of the Department of Naval Intelligence that he needed a photograph of a young woman to put in with others to see if a witness could identify a suspected spy. One of the women gladly gave her own picture for this purpose. She became Pam, the major's fiancée.

After having another woman write two love letters to Major Martin, Montagu spent a good deal of time folding, unfolding, and rubbing them against his clothing so the letters would look as if the major had read and reread them, as a man in love might do.

It was not hard to get an invitation from a London nightclub to suggest that the major liked a good time. And Montagu bought tickets to a London show for April 22, carefully tearing off the stubs as if the major had used them only a few days before he died.

A letter from J. G. Martin, the major's father, revealed that he had been making plans to give his son a large sum of money in view of his upcoming marriage. The letter was written on the official stationery of the Black Lion, a well-known resort hotel. This letter included some private family details and made reference to an unattractive cousin the team made up.

"Your cousin Priscilla asked to be remembered to you," the letter read. "She has grown into a sensible girl, though I cannot say that her work for the Land Army has done much to improve her looks. In that respect I am afraid that she will take after her father's side of the family."

The team went to great trouble to add these personal touches. They knew that the Germans would be suspicious of the body and would be on the lookout for signs of a trick. Every item to be found was developed with the greatest care.

Someone suggested that Major Martin should not appear to be too perfect. He ought to have one fault, at least. Without explaining their purpose, the team was able to get a letter from Lloyds Bank in London, a notice demanding that the major pay a debt he had neglected even after several reminders. This letter was actually signed by the manager and was added to the personal papers to indicate that although the major was a nice enough fellow, he could be careless about a debt.

Even in the secret papers carried in the black briefcase, there were friendly personal comments. Lord Louis Mountbatten, chief of combined operations, was in on the secret of Operation Mincemeat. He personally wrote a letter addressed to Sir Andrew Cunningham, commander in chief of Allied forces in the Mediterranean.

"I think," Lord Mountbatten wrote in introducing the major, "you will find Martin the man you want. He is quiet and shy àt first, but he really knows his stuff."

In April of 1943, the final approval for Operation Mincemeat was given by Prime Minister Winston Churchill, who thought the Allies had nothing to lose and everything to gain by it. Montagu and his team prepared Major Martin for his mission. The body was taken out of cold storage and dressed in a Royal Marines uniform.

The team filled the major's pockets with personal effects and papers. They locked the black briefcase with the official letters inside and fastened it by a chain through the major's sleeve. This was not the usual way that officers carried secret papers, but the team had to take a chance that the Germans would not know this or question the method. After all, it would not do to have the briefcase float away in the water and not be found.

A long, cylindrical canister marked "Optical Instruments" and packed with dry ice waited for the major's stiff body. The team slipped the corpse inside and poured more dry ice over it to keep the body frozen. Montagu himself and two of his men delivered the canister to the commanding officer of the submarine *Seraph*, a Lieutenant Jewell. At first, the lieutenant was the only member of the crew who knew what the canister really contained.

On April 30, the four sailors Lieutenant Jewell chose

to help him launch the body were astonished and shaken to learn what their mission really was. In the dark hours before dawn, the submarine surfaced off the coast of Huelva and Major Martin was launched into the water along with a rubber lifeboat floating upside down to suggest an accident.

Moved by what they were doing, and out of respect for the dead, the lieutenant recited prayers from the burial service as Major Martin went off on his mission.

Later on April 30, 1943, a Spanish fisherman was at work in the Mediterranean Sea off the coast of Spain when he was startled by a large form in the water near his boat. The object was too big and too ominously still to be a fish. Cautiously, the fisherman drew close enough to investigate.

The body of a man in military uniform and encased in a life preserver from shoulder to waist rode on the tide toward shore. One of the dead man's hands was curled around a black briefcase, as if his last conscious thought had been to protect its precious contents.

For a moment, the fisherman hesitated, wondering what secrets the case might hold and whether they might be valuable to him, but the ghoulish sight made him shudder and he rowed away. He hailed the first government launch he saw and described what he had found.

Three days later, the British learned from Spanish officials that the body of a Royal Marine had been found floating in Spanish waters not far from the village of Huelva.

The Royal Marine, the Spanish reported, appeared to be the victim of an airplane crash at sea and had been dead about five days. There was no mention of a black briefcase.

On May 4, Major Martin was buried in Huelva Cemetery with military honors befitting an officer who died during wartime. Pam and the family sent a large wreath for his grave.

On the day of Major Martin's funeral, British agents in Huelva received an urgent message from London inquiring about the briefcase and asking that the top-secret papers it contained be recovered without arousing suspicion. Montagu had sent this communication deliberately to arouse interest in the contents of the briefcase. The message from London, which Montague hoped would be intercepted by the Germans, said that these letters were so important not even the British officials in Spain were to open and read them.

All the team could do then was wait. Would the Spanish open and read the letters? Would the information they contained be discovered by the German spy Montagu was counting on?

It was not until the black briefcase was returned nine days later that the team knew for certain the secret papers inside had been opened. The team had taken special precautions in sealing the envelopes so they could tell at once if those seals had been broken. They had been.

Montagu lost no time in sending a triumphant message to Prime Minister Churchill: "Mincemeat Swallowed Whole!"

In the weeks that followed the discovery of the briefcase, the Germans went into action reorganizing their military forces. Convinced that the Allies now planned to invade Europe through Greece, Hitler ordered his military leaders to make preparations. The first German Panzer division, which included crack German troops and their tanks, were moved to Greece, as were German motor torpedo boats.

On July 10, 1943, the Allied forces landed in Sicily, where the Allied soldiers met little German resistance because the largest German forces were waiting in Greece for the huge attack that did not come.

The Germans had been taken in by Major Martin. The many Allied soldiers who survived the successful invasion of Sicily that July had Lieutenant Commander Ewen Montagu and his heroic team of dedicated counterspies to thank for creating "The Man Who Never Was" and feeding the German spies information they were only too anxious to steal and believe.

▲ 9 ▲

The Clenched Fist

In the hour before midnight, George Wood stood amid the shadows in the middle of a bridge that spanned the Aare River in Switzerland. He had been instructed to wait for a car that would signal him with its fender lights.

There was not much traffic on the bridge, but each time a car approached, George Wood drew deeper into the shadows. His dark clothing, his leather jacket, and the black hat that covered his balding head made him nearly invisible. Still, someone in an oncoming car might notice him.

Once this mission was complete, Wood wondered, would he find the courage to try another? Every sound, every movement struck fear into his heart. Another car turned onto the bridge and Wood shrank back. Faint blue fender lights flashed quickly and the car came to a stop not ten feet away.

Was this a trick or was it his contact? Now or never, Wood thought, and he stepped from the shadows.

Once inside the car, he breathed a shaky sigh of relief.

"Welcome back, George," the driver said. "I hope your trip was not too difficult." The driver was Gerald Mayer, assistant to the chief of the American OSS, the Office of Strategic Services.

Wood only grunted. Despite his American-sounding name, George Wood was German, a spy within Hitler's foreign office who was feeding secret information to the Allies. Actually, the trip from Berlin had been nerve-racking.

Wood, whose real name was Fritz Kolbe, was carrying secret documents he had photographed and smuggled into Switzerland. Getting the secret papers past the German and Swiss inspectors at the border took ingenuity. Kolbe was carrying a diplomatic pouch for the German office in Bern, Switzerland. Diplomatic pouches were never opened by inspectors. He had put an envelope of official diplomatic documents and his two hundred pages of stolen papers inside a larger envelope and then had sealed everything with red tape and a large swastika.

The moment he passed the border, he rushed into the men's room of the railroad station, put the secret papers into his pockets, and flushed the larger envelope down the toilet, leaving the real diplomatic papers in their original envelope. He delivered this envelope to the German embassy in Bern. Now he was anxious to get rid of the military secrets before anyone discovered what he had done.

Dr. Fritz Kolbe thought he should have gotten used

to living with fear, but he never did. For twenty years, he had been working in Berlin for the German Foreign Service. When the Nazis came to power, with Adolf Hitler as their leader, Kolbe's job was to sort through secret messages from German agents all over the world for his superior, Karl Ritter, assistant to Joachim von Ribbentrop, Hitler's foreign minister. The more Kolbe learned about Hitler and what the Nazis were doing, the more he hated them.

Kolbe decided it was foolish to be silently angry.

"It is not enough to clench your fist and hide it in your pocket," he told a friend. "The fist must be used to strike."

The only way to save his country was to get rid of Hitler and the Nazis forever, Kolbe reasoned. He decided to contact someone in the British government. The British, the French, and the Americans were working together as the Allies against Germany, who led the Axis powers during World War II.

Switzerland was the place to make such a contact because it was a neutral country. Kolbe arranged through a friend to make contact with an official at the British embassy when the time came. But the time did not come until the summer of 1943.

A year earlier, Kolbe had asked his superiors if he could take a vacation in the Alps. The request was denied with no explanation. Kolbe was worried. Did the Nazis suspect his intentions? The Gestapo were clever, and they seemed to be everywhere. But even the risk of discovery did not stop Kolbe. He waited and continued to collect secret documents.

Every day, valuable information crossed his desk — information that the Allies could use to defeat Hitler. Kolbe had to come up with a plan that would not arouse suspicion.

After a year, he thought it was safe to try to leave the country again, if only he could think of a clever way. He knew that pouches containing government papers were carried regularly by messengers or couriers from Berlin to German offices in neutral countries. At last, a solution came to him that was so simple, he wondered why he had not thought of it sooner.

The assistant chief of the courier section in his office was a woman named Maria von Heimerdinger. She was a member of an old, noble German family. Dr. Kolbe often thought she felt the same way he did about Hitler and the Nazi party, but he did not dare ask her. One day, he told Maria that he had to take care of some business interests in Switzerland. It was not unusual for Germans to have business interests in Switzerland, a country known for its banking. He asked her if she thought it would be possible for him to deliver one of the diplomatic pouches there.

Maria asked no questions.

"There is a pouch to be delivered to Bern soon. I can arrange to have you carry that if you like," she said.

Dr. Kolbe did not become careless, however. He took

all the secret material he had been collecting and strapped it to his leg. Carrying the diplomatic pouch, which was sealed with a red swastika, he boarded the train for Switzerland. Throughout the eighteen-hour trip, Kolbe hardly slept. He was prepared to destroy all his secret material if there was any trouble. To be caught smuggling secrets out of Germany would mean certain death, but nothing happened.

In Bern, he delivered the pouch to the Germans and then went to the British embassy, where his old business friend Dr. Ernesto Kocherthaler had made an appointment for him with a Colonel Cartwright.

Kolbe was nervous during the interview. He did not like the way the intelligence officer stared at him in stony silence. What was Colonel Cartwright thinking? Kolbe was a short, robust German with thinning blond hair that looked like a halo around his bald head. He sat stiffly on the edge of his straight-backed chair and began to tell his story. His words and phrases came out in an excited rush as he tried to make the colonel see how valuable his information could be.

When Dr. Kolbe had finished, the British officer shook his head and stared at him coldly. He would not even look at any of the papers Kolbe had brought.

"I don't believe you. Not a word of it," the colonel said. "And if it is all true, then you're a cad."

Kolbe was unceremoniously shown from the office. Feeling insulted and discouraged, he returned to his hotel room. But after a time, he could understand the

British attitude. They must suspect him of being part of a Nazi trick. That was only natural.

Finally, Kolbe went outside to one of the enclosed phone booths in the street. He did not dare use the phone in his room to make another contact. There were many Germans staying in the hotels and he could not assume that his phone call would be private.

Kolbe called Dr. Kocherthaler, who agreed to contact the Americans for him. The next day, Kocherthaler went to see Gerald Mayer, the assistant to Allen Dulles, who was chief of the OSS. He told Mayer about Kolbe and showed Mayer some of the secret papers. One of them reported plans to infiltrate German spies in the Balkan countries. Another was a message from Paris, describing how German spies could be moved through American and British lines in North Africa. Each of the messages was marked "Geheime Reichsache" — Secret State Document.

Mayer was so impressed that he went to his chief for advice. Chief Dulles agreed to meet with Kolbe and Mayer that very evening. It was August 24, 1943. Before midnight, Chief Dulles was as impressed with Kolbe as Mayer was.

Again, Dr. Kolbe sat stiffly in a chair, holding the leather case containing the German Foreign Service secrets. He was just as nervous with the Americans as he had been with the British, but somehow he kept himself from speaking too fast.

Finally, Dulles asked to see the papers. There was

silence in the room as he examined them. That summer, the Germans had been weakened by American
and British bombing raids. But the Americans needed
to know just how strong the Germans still were, what
their military production was like, and where they
planned to strike next. Kolbe was in a perfect position
to feed the Americans this information. There were
some answers to these questions in the 186 separate
secrets Kolbe had produced. Still, the Americans were
cautious.

Dulles, who had been smoking his pipe, set it in an
ashtray, leaned forward, and asked Kolbe the question
that had been bothering him. He needed to know the
man's motive before he could begin to trust him.

"Why would you want to do this? Why would you
betray your country?"

A fierce anger flashed in Kolbe's eyes.

"I do not betray my country," he said. "I hate the
Nazis. They are destroying my country. I want nothing
in return for this work except to see Hitler defeated,"
he finished, looking directly at Dulles.

Dulles, who had called himself "Mr. Douglas" as a
precaution, gazed steadily back, and Kolbe saw ac-
ceptance in the American's expression. Of course, Mr.
Douglas and his assistant would want to check Kolbe's
story carefully. Kolbe gave them all the information
they would need to do that.

It was nearly dawn when the meeting broke up. All
the next day, Dulles and Mayer went over the documents Kolbe had delivered. Some of them were sent

on to Washington and even reached President Franklin Roosevelt. Dr. Fritz Kolbe was officially taken on as an American agent and was assigned the code name of George Wood.

Kolbe's career as a spy inside the Nazi regime nearly came to an end when he returned to Berlin. He was summoned to his superior's office, where he learned that his movements in Bern had been monitored. The Germans had noticed he was not in his hotel room on the night of August 24.

"Account for your time," he was ordered.

Kolbe's heart nearly froze in his chest, but he thought to invent a girlfriend and said he had been visiting her. His superior officer was not pleased, but he seemed to believe the alibi.

Kolbe went back to his office trembling, but the close call did not stop him from photographing and collecting material for the Americans. He made a copy of every secret document that crossed his desk. He made notes of important meetings involving Hitler's inner circle of military officers as well. He had to find safe places to use his microfilm camera and often used the basement of a nearby hospital. One night, he was in the midst of photographing a file when he heard that von Ribbentrop and Heinrich Himmler, Hitler's right hand, wanted to see that very file at once. Kolbe raced from the hospital through the streets of Berlin to his office, pretended to rummage in the files, and then produced the file he had had in his pocket all the while.

On his second visit to Bern, Kolbe alerted the Americans to the news that the Germans knew when a large convoy of ships and servicemen was leaving an American port. The Germans were preparing to meet and destroy the convoy with their U-boats. Luckily for the Allies, Kolbe's information reached the Americans in time and the U-boats waited in vain. Kolbe thus saved thousands of American lives. Kolbe also reported a serious leak in British intelligence: at the British embassy in Turkey, the ambassador's valet was a German spy whose code name was Cicero.

Dulles remembered the girlfriend Kolbe had invented to fool his superiors after his first trip to Switzerland. He told Kolbe she might send him messages when some important information was needed. Once, Kolbe received a postcard that read: "Perhaps you remember my friend's little son. His birthday is coming soon and I wanted to get him some of those clever Japanese toys with which the shops here used to be full, but I can't find any. I wonder if there might be some left in Berlin." This was signed "Emmy."

Kolbe quickly realized the Americans were asking for information on Japanese military plans and naval strength. When he carried his next pouch to Bern, he carried that information too.

Month after month, George Wood continued to feed Nazi secrets to the Americans. He knew his work was valuable, but when Kolbe learned that a number of his friends were involved in a plot to kill Hitler, he wanted to become a part of this underground group. On his next trip to Switzerland, Wood told Chief Dulles about his plan.

Dulles was distressed. "I don't think you have any idea what your reports have meant to us. Please reconsider. Your value as a spy is unsurpassed. And what if the plot to kill Hitler fails? You would certainly be killed yourself."

"It won't fail," Kolbe argued.

"But the risk is there. You are a highly skilled agent. We could never replace you. Why waste that skill? No one else can do what you are doing to defeat Hitler. Let the others carry out the plan. We need you, George."

Although George Wood argued stubbornly, he finally gave in.

On July 20, 1944, a bomb exploded right under a table where Hitler was supposed to have been sitting, but he escaped harm. The Nazis rounded up the men involved in the conspiracy and killed them. Luckily, Kolbe was not among them. He went on doing what he could to undermine the Nazis until he, too, had to escape to Switzerland for safety.

Fritz Kolbe's work as a spy was over, but his heroism would never be forgotten. He was a true hero who asked nothing for his work but the satisfaction of having contributed to the victory over an evil dictator he saw ruining his homeland. It was this honorable motive that helped Chief Dulles make up his mind about Fritz Kolbe. Dulles saw in him one of the most valuable agents on his team.

After World War II came to an end, Dr. Fritz Kolbe testified against the Nazi officers at the war crimes trial in Nuremberg. Only then did the Nazis learn that he was George Wood, the successful spy whose clenched fist had struck again and again, adding to the blows that destroyed Hitler's power and saved the Germany that Kolbe loved.

▲ 10 ▲

The Third Man

Stewart Menzies sat in his office in London reading and rereading the message that had just arrived from Istanbul, wondering what to make of the news that there were three important Communist spies in London. As chief of the British Secret Intelligence Service, SIS, that summer of 1945, Menzies was ready for almost any kind of treachery from the Russians.

Although the Soviet Union was Britain's ally during World War II, it was increasingly clear that once the Germans and Japanese surrendered, the world faced a new danger from the East. From the time of their 1917 revolution in Russia, the Communists had never been interested in making the world safe for democracy. The worst of it was that the Communists worked from within, persuading trusted British and American officials — even intelligence officers — to join them in building the Communist world.

This was a new kind of war, a "cold war" in which soldiers did not fight each other on battlefields. Instead, the enemy gained victories by stealing secrets and murdering those who got in the way of their plans.

Menzies's hands shook with anger as he read the long message again. It had been handwritten and hand-delivered instead of being sent in code by telegraph. It told a bizarre story.

A few days earlier, a short, stocky Russian had arrived at the British embassy in Turkey.

"I must see your highest official," he said, his words difficult to understand through his heavy Russian accent.

He was introduced to a diplomat, who offered to call in an interpreter, but the Russian refused to have a third person present during their interview.

"I need no interpreter. I speak well enough," the man said in his halting English.

The Russian told his story, lowering his voice to a confidential half-whisper.

"I am Konstantin Volkov. You know my name?"

"Yes, of course, sir. You're the new Russian consul," the British diplomat said.

"I am more. I am with Soviet intelligence and I have information to sell."

He handed a sheaf of papers to the Brtitish diplomat, who tried to contain his surprise when he realized he was looking at floor plans and details of the alarm system in the offices of the Soviet intelligence headquarters in Moscow. There was also a list of Russian spies in Turkey, with their addresses and the identifying numbers of their cars.

"I have more," Volkov said.

"More?"

"There are three Communist agents in your country in high positions, two in the foreign office in London and one in intelligence. You are interested in the identities of these Russian spies?"

"Yes, yes, of course," the diplomat assured him quickly, finding it hard to hide his shock. Who could these three traitors be?

Volkov nodded. "I will sell all to you for twenty-seven thousand pounds and permission to go to Cyprus. You agree?"

Cyprus was a British-controlled island in the Mediterranean. Obviously, Volkov wanted to escape from the Russians and his work as a spy.

The British diplomat was as encouraging as possible.

"We are very interested, but I'm afraid I can't give you an answer right away. The matter must be approved in London, you see. We cannot take responsibility for this matter here in Turkey. I'm sure you understand."

Volkov's dark eyes were like stones in his gray face. He said nothing. He was trying to hide his nervousness with his gruff manner. If the Russians ever learned that he was willing to betray his own people, his life would be worth nothing.

"I will wait twenty-one days only," Volkov said. "You

will send your request to London handwritten and by courier. Use no code, no telegraph. There is an enemy agent in your embassy. I cannot risk to have the message typed."

"Who? What agent?" the diplomat demanded.

Volkov shook his head.

"When we have our deal, I will tell you. I will go now. Twenty-one days," he warned.

After Volkov left, the diplomat sat for hours recording by hand what had happened, just as the Russian had directed. The moment his report was ready, he sent it out. But it was several days before the courier arrived in London and presented it to Chief Menzies.

The intelligence chief read the message a third time. He could not imagine anyone among his friends at the foreign office or on his own staff being a Communist agent.

But if what this Volkov said was true, much of the intelligence work at the SIS had been for nothing. The Russians must know all their secrets.

I will have someone look into this matter at once, thought Menzies, someone I can trust.

He sent for Harold Adrian Russell Philby, whose friends called him Kim because he had been born in India like the boy hero of Rudyard Kipling's book of that name.

As a high-ranking member of British intelligence, Philby was in charge of British double agents and of passing false information to the Russians.

"What do you make of this, Philby?" Chief Menzies

asked as he pushed the handwritten pages across his desk.

Philby seldom showed emotion. He was a quiet, shy man who stuttered whether he was nervous or not, but he was a crack intelligence officer. He read the pages carefully.

"I d-don't know wh-what to th-think," Philby said, meeting Menzies's concerned gaze with one of his own.

"Could it be true? I mean, three such spies, so well placed?" Menzies prodded.

"It's h-hard to say, sir. I'd like to m-meet this Volkov."

"Just what I was thinking. Take personal charge of the matter, will you, Philby?"

Philby was glad Menzies had chosen him for this assignment. Some time later, he left for Istanbul and arrived twenty-one days after Volkov's unexpected visit to the embassy. He met the British diplomat who had spoken with Volkov.

"Couldn't you have made it any sooner?" the diplomat demanded angrily. "I sent you two requests. Didn't you get them? Volkov only gave us twenty-one days."

"Well, old b-boy, it c-couldn't be helped and this day isn't over yet, is it?" Philby said. He suggested that the diplomat try to contact Volkov so they could get on with the deal.

Discouraged and afraid they had waited too long, the embassy official did as he was told. They waited all day for an answer from Volkov. As evening approached, it was clear that they would never hear from him.

Perhaps the news of Volkov's offer had leaked out somehow. The diplomat did not like to think what could have happened to the Russian informer, and he blamed Philby for not acting faster.

Several weeks later, a Russian military plane unexpectedly flew into Istanbul airport. Before anyone could do anything about this aircraft, a car sped onto the runway. In a flash, a stretcher carrying a heavily bandaged body was carried from the car and placed aboard the plane, which took off immediately.

The British suspected the bandaged man was Volkov. The Russians must have found out about him and taken their revenge. Everyone knew how harshly Russians dealt with traitors.

Some time later, the British diplomat told an intelligence officer what he thought of Kim Philby, who was then being considered for a higher position. There were even rumors he would someday take Menzies's place as chief of SIS.

"You can say what you like about him, but I think he's a dangerous man. Either he's hopelessly incompetent or a Russian spy. He might as well have murdered Volkov himself."

The words were said in anger, but the diplomat had put his finger on the truth.

Kim Philby became a Communist in 1931, along with a number of other students at Cambridge in those days. All through the war years, he had worked in

British intelligence, passing along information to the Russians and identifying British spies so they could be caught and killed. At the time of the Volkov incident, Philby, along with two agents in the foreign office, had crippled much of the work of British intelligence. They planned to do even more because the balance of power in the cold war was not in favor of the Russians.

President Harry S. Truman had given a clear statement of what he thought of the Russians in August of 1945 when he decided not to share the atomic bomb with them: "The atomic bomb is too dangerous to be loose in a lawless world. That is why Great Britain and the United States, who have the secret of its production, do not intend to reveal the secret until means have been found to control the bomb so as to protect ourselves and the rest of the world from total destruction."

The atomic bomb made the Americans and the English the most powerful people in the world. There was only one thing for the Communists to do: steal the bomb and as many other military secrets as they could to even the balance of power.

One of Philby's college friends, Donald Maclean, was sent by the British foreign office to work in Washington, D.C. Maclean was so well liked and trusted by the British and the Americans that he was invited to sit in on Atomic Energy Commission meetings. He reported everything he heard to his Russian contacts.

Another of Philby's college friends was Guy Burgess, who worked in the foreign office in London. For years, he had been gathering secrets and passing them along to the Communists. And in his high position inside the SIS, Philby was able to do even more damage to British spies inside Communist countries.

When Philby heard about Volkov's offer to identify the three Communist agents, he was terrified. "It was the worst moment of my life," he later confessed.

But he learned about Volkov before Volkov could act. Philby tipped off the Russians, then took his time traveling to Istanbul. By then, the Russians had captured Volkov and silenced him. Philby, Burgess, and Maclean were safe again.

Philby went right on being the affable member of the SIS team. His charm won him many powerful friends, Menzies among them. Everyone liked the gentle, unassuming Philby, who never forgot birthdays or special occasions and would even go into debt for a friend in need. Soon, his suspicious behavior in the Volkov incident was all but forgotten.

Four years later, in 1949, Philby was assigned to an important post in Washington, D.C. He was working closely with the Federal Bureau of Investigation and the Central Intelligence Agency — the FBI and the CIA. Philby met regularly with a Communist contact outside the city to pass along all he learned. By this time, Donald Maclean was back in London, but Philby's old college friend and fellow Communist Guy Burgess was soon to be in Washington too.

"Could you put me up, old boy?" Burgess wrote Philby.

Philby did not mind having Burgess stay at his house while he was in Washington, but Philby's wife was upset.

"Not Guy Burgess! He's so vulgar and loud. He drinks too much. I don't like him around the children," protested Aileen Philby, who had no idea of the treacherous double lives Philby, Burgess, and Maclean were leading.

"N-nonsense, m-my dear," Philby said. "The children are very fond of him. What other gr-grown man will sit right down on the floor with them and p-play with their trains?"

The Philbys had four children and it was true they adored Burgess. But Philby knew his wife was right about his old college friend, who often acted irresponsibly and had been getting into trouble in London lately. Philby thought it would be a good idea to have Burgess close by, where he could keep an eye on him.

Aileen Philby made room for Burgess in their house, but it was not long before Burgess was in trouble with the British at the embassy and the Americans as well.

The first thing Burgess did when he came to Washington was buy a huge, white Lincoln sedan, which he drove around the city and the countryside so recklessly that he soon had a large collection of traffic tickets — which he simply ignored.

"I have diplomatic immunity," Burgess said when Philby questioned him about his behavior. "American laws mean nothing to me and the police can't arrest me. What's the use of having immunity if you can't have a little fun?" he said and went on making a nuisance of himself at diplomatic receptions and on the road.

When the governor of Virginia sent a formal protest to the British embassy, it was clear that Burgess's days as a diplomat were numbered. Surely, he'd be fired.

It was at this time that Philby came across a disturbing piece of information in an FBI file. The Americans were investigating the identity of a Communist spy who had worked in the British embassy in Washington a few years earlier. Four names were listed and one of them was Donald Maclean. It was only a matter of time before the Americans found Maclean out. Philby was worried.

"We've got t-to warn him," Philby told Burgess.

This was as dangerous as the Volkov incident. Maclean had a history of nervous breakdowns. He would never stand up under questioning.

"Don't worry, old man," Burgess said. "I'm about to be sacked anyway. I'll leave now and get to him in time."

But Burgess was as irresponsible as ever. He did not rush back to London by plane, but instead cruised back on the *Queen Mary*, which sailed from New York and arrived in London days later, on May 7, 1951.

Philby was beside himself with worry. Every day, he saw the British and the Americans closing in on

Maclean. And still there was no word from Burgess about plans to get Maclean out of the country.

When Philby learned that in only four days the British planned to question Maclean, he knew he had to warn Burgess to hurry. He sent a telegram with a message about the Lincoln Burgess had left parked in the diplomatic parking lot. He said if Burgess did not do something about it at once, it would be sent to the scrap heap.

To anyone else, the message would have seemed harmless, but to Burgess it was the push he needed. He realized that the Lincoln really referred to Maclean. Suddenly, Burgess and Maclean vanished from London. They turned up in Russia some months later.

Everyone in London, including Maclean's wife, was astonished and sorry to learn that Maclean and Burgess were Russian spies. In Washington, Bedell Smith, head of the CIA, was angry. Someone had told Burgess to warn Maclean so the two Soviet spies could escape. Although Smith had no way of proving it, he suspected Philby was the third man — a third Communist agent, the only person who knew enough to warn Burgess. Smith refused to work with Philby anymore and demanded that he be recalled. As a result, Philby lost his job in military intelligence and had little hope of being trusted to hold such a sensitive position again.

Much to the disgust of the Americans, Philby was not arrested or accused of anything. He had too many friends who believed in him and who could not see beneath his "good-old-boy" disguise to the Russian spy underneath.

For a time, Philby worked at odd jobs, but then someone got him a position on a newspaper in Beirut, Lebanon. He was in Beirut six years when a Russian agent defected and finally revealed the whole Burgess-Maclean story and identified Philby as the third man.

Nicholas Elliott of the Secret Intelligence Service, an old friend of Philby's, volunteered to go to Beirut and bring him home.

Elliott arrived in January 1963. He and Philby had lunch together and Elliott told Philby what the SIS had learned.

"I once looked up to you, Kim," he said. "How I despise you now. I hope you've enough decency left to understand why," Elliott told him with deep feeling.

He was surprised at how quickly Philby gave up and confessed that he was a Soviet spy. Philby even agreed to sign a confession — but he did not agree to go back to London right away and turn against the Russians. He said he needed time to think. Elliott could not arrest Philby in a foreign country, but being a gentleman himself, he expected Philby to act like a gentleman too and keep his word. Elliott went home, assuming that Philby would follow.

Philby had two choices. He could either go back home and face the charges against him or he could run away. There was not really any point in staying in Beirut. Once his friends found out, they would have nothing to do with him.

On January 23, 1963, Philby was on his way to a dinner party in a taxi when he asked the driver to pull over.

"I've forgotten an important matter, information I must ship out today. I won't be long," he said, but he never came back and he never arrived at the party.

Some time later, the Russian government announced Philby was in the Soviet Union. For twenty-five years, until he died in May of 1988, Philby went on living there, knowing he could never return to England.

Did Philby have regrets? He said he did not because England was never his home.

"I was born in India, brought up in various parts of the Arab world, and I was at school in England. I don't feel that I have any nationality," he told friends.

This statement may be the key to his philosophy. As a student, he decided Communism was the form of government that would make the world a better place and he was willing to take enormous risks to help the cause. In that sense, he might be judged a hero by some, but the treachery of the third man will never be forgotten by the Western world.

▲ 11 ▲

The Spy Next Door

James Bozarts knew the value of money. He was thirteen and a responsible newspaper boy in Brooklyn, New York. On a warm summer day in 1953, James was making his rounds, collecting money from his customers.

Suddenly, one of the coins slipped from his fingers. James bent to pick it up, caught his breath, and stared in astonishment. The nickel was in two pieces, as if it had been sliced in half through its rim, so there were now two flat circles. Inside one of the circles was a tiny piece of film. James had never seen anything like this before.

His parents were just as surprised as he was, but they had heard about the new way messages could be photographed and reduced to such a degree that a tiny black microdot, no bigger than the dot of an *i*, could contain a whole page of information. Spies often used microfilm and microdots to record secrets and smuggle them out of the country. The Bozarts turned the nickel and the microfilm over to the local police, who passed everything along to the FBI.

The tiny film contained a set of numbers. Try as they would, the FBI agents were unable to crack the complicated code. They suspected the message had been sent from one spy to another. Since the FBI could not identify these spies at the moment, there was nothing to do but wait for new information to turn up. The agents waited four years before they learned that the key to the mystery was right across the street.

The offices of the FBI in Brooklyn were located on Fulton Street. In the building across the way, a number of artists rented studios. Emil R. Goldfuss was one of these artists.

Emil was a slim, quiet man who wore glasses. People who saw him on the street hardly gave the balding man a second glance. He was a painter and a photographer who spoke English with a slight Irish accent. He owned a small library of books and could talk for hours about art, literature, nuclear science, and even the theory of numbers. His hobby was working with a shortwave radio whose aerial he had placed on the roof of his building.

Many of Emil's friends visited him in his studio, which was lined with the paintings he had produced since he moved to Brooklyn in 1948. His neighbors found him a courteous man and the superintendent of his building was grateful for Emil's help in repairing the elevator one day.

No one suspected that Emil R. Goldfuss was really the cover name for an important Russian spy, Rudolf Ivañovich Abel. But even the best spy makes mistakes, and Abel made one that ended his career.

In 1927, Rudolf Abel was twenty-five years old and had completed his espionage training in Russia. He carried out several successful assignments that impressed his superiors. In World War II, he even managed to masquerade as a German and became part of the Nazi Secret Service, gathering valuable information. After the war, in 1947, the Russians needed a new man to take charge of their agents in New York City. Colonel Rudolf Abel was chosen.

Abel came into Canada on a forged passport in the name of Andrew Kayotis. From Canada, he traveled to Brooklyn and became Emil R. Goldfuss. He even had a birth certificate to prove his identity. There had been an Emil Goldfuss born in New York, but he had died as a baby over forty years before.

For the first few years in America, Abel did nothing but establish himself in the community, making friends with artists in Brooklyn and setting up his art-and-photography studio.

Then he began his work as a spy. When he wished to send a message to one of his agents or arrange a meeting, he would first translate the information into a series of numbers. These he photographed with special equipment so that the message would fit into tiny spaces like the coin James Bozarts found. Using delicate instruments, Abel hollowed out other ordinary objects, such as cuff links and screws, so he could place filmed messages inside. Sometimes, he reduced messages to microdots, hid these dots in the spines of magazines, and sent them to agents in other countries.

To his agents, Abel was not known as Emil Goldfuss. These spies used his code name, Mark. Code names protected the true identity of agents. If a spy decided to defect and tell all he knew to the Americans, it would be hard for him to identify other members of the Russian spy network.

Abel might have continued stealing American military secrets indefinitely if it had not been for his new assistant, Reino Hayhanen. Hayhanen, who arrived in America in 1952 after living and working for the Russians in Finland, went by the code name Vic. Abel never knew exactly where "Vic" lived. This was another rule for Russian agents in America. The spies all met away from their homes or businesses. Again, this step was taken to keep the spies from knowing too much about each other.

When Abel first met his new assistant in 1954, he was surprised that Hayhanen's English was so poor. The man spoke with such a heavy accent that it was hard for him to fit into an American community without drawing attention to himself. The first order Abel gave Hayhanen was to improve his English, and the second was to brush up on his codes, many of which he had forgotten.

For nearly a year, Abel and Hayhanen worked together. Abel showed his assistant the places the spy network used as "letter boxes." These were spots where messages could be left by one spy and picked up by another. In Prospect Park in Brooklyn, for instance, there was a broken spot in some concrete steps where a hollow screw containing microfilm might be placed. Abel showed Hayhanen how to set up a radio transmitter for sending messages to other countries, and they traveled around looking for the best places to send out signals.

In 1955, Abel was recalled to Moscow. He had earned a six-month vacation to visit his wife and daughter. Hayhanen, as Abel's assistant, was left in charge of the spy network.

When Abel returned, he was not pleased with what he found. Hayhanen had been neglecting his work. Other spies complained that Hayhanen had not been collecting messages from the "letter boxes."

Abel reported what he had learned to his superiors in Moscow and Hayhanen was asked to return home for a "rest." Suspicious that he was in trouble, Hayhanen only pretended to leave for Russia. Instead, he went to the American embassy in Paris. There, he offered to tell the Americans all he knew about the Russian spy network in New York. In exchange, he asked the Americans to give him protection and allow him to go on living in America.

It was not easy for Hayhanen to come up with information that would lead the FBI to Abel because Hayhanen did not know exactly where Abel lived or what name he was using. But the Americans were patient. They asked Hayhanen to tell them everything he knew. Even the slightest bit of information might be helpful. Finally, Hayhanen remembered something crucial.

Once, Abel had taken his assistant to a storeroom he rented between Clark and Fulton streets in Brooklyn. This was the mistake that ended Abel's career. The FBI found the storeroom, which had been rented by Emil R. Goldfuss in the same building in which he lived — right across the street from FBI headquarters. The description the superintendent of the building had given of Goldfuss fit the description Hayhanen had given of "Mark."

All the agents had to do was wait for Goldfuss to return from a trip to Florida, where he had told the superintendent he had gone on vacation. While they waited, the agents remembered the mysterious nickel and film James Bozarts had found. Hayhanen recognized the code on the film at once and translated it for them.

The message, he agreed, was probably meant for him since it had been discovered soon after his arrival in America. It began:

1. We congratulate you on a safe arrival. We confirm the receipt of your letter to the address "V" repeat "V" and the reading of letter Number 1.

2. For organization of cover, we gave instructions to transmit to you three thousand in local currency.

It was a while before Colonel Abel returned to his Fulton Street studio. He had been alerted to some kind of trouble when Hayhanen did not show up in Moscow. Abel took the precaution of changing his name to Marvin Collins and found another place to live, but he finally did come back to pick up some equipment. The FBI agents were keeping a close watch and spotted him.

On October 14, 1957, Colonel Rudolf Abel was charged with conspiring to steal secret military information from the United States and with illegal entry into the country. Anyone brought to trial in America has the right to a defense attorney, even a Russian spy. Colonel Abel was represented by James Donovan, a distinguished lawyer and a loyal American. Despite their political differences, Donovan gave Colonel Abel the best defense he could. Donovan argued that some of the evidence against Colonel Abel had been obtained illegally — without a search warrant, contrary to one of the rights guaranteed by the United States Constitution.

But Hayhanen's testimony and the discovery of all the spying equipment in Abel's studio and storeroom convinced the jury of Abel's guilt. Even the Supreme Court later upheld the jury's decision. The problem was how Abel should be sentenced. The charge for conspiring to steal military secrets called for the death penalty.

Donovan argued that the judge ought to take into consideration the fact that the United States and Russia were not at war. He also reasoned that to protect itself the United States was also making every effort to learn Russian military secrets too.

"Who knows," he said, "that at some later date an American might not fall into Russian hands, charged with similar offenses? If Colonel Abel is then still alive, maybe it will be possible to effect an exchange of prisoners."

The judge sentenced Colonel Abel to thirty years in prison.

Two years later, an American pilot was flying a mission in a jet aircraft that was so remarkable it could fly higher than any aircraft had ever flown before. It was called a Utility-2 plane — or U-2, for short. The pilot, Francis Gary Powers, had been flying secret missions over Russia for four years, checking on Soviet missile bases and other military activities.

Because the plane could fly as high as seventy thousand feet, it was out of reach of Russian fighter planes and ordinary antiaircraft weapons. The U-2 plane carried special cameras that could photograph sites from such heights. Powers was trained to use this equipment.

But on May 1, 1960, the Russians managed to bring the U-2 plane, piloted by Powers, to the ground, not far from the Russian industrial city of Sverdlovsk. Both the plane and the pilot were captured. Many people at the time criticized Powers for not destroying his plane and doing away with himself so he could not be questioned by the Russians.

But unlike Colonel Abel, Powers had not been

trained as a spy. He was a skillful pilot who operated a sophisticated spy plane. This was a new kind of espionage and new rules had to be applied. Powers did what he was instructed to do. He told the Russians no more than they already knew. Even President Dwight Eisenhower admitted to the world that the Americans had been spying. Powers did not try to deny this or anything else that was obviously true.

In August of 1960, there was a trial in Moscow and Powers was convicted of spying. Like Abel, he was not sentenced to death.

Nearly two years later, Colonel Rudolf Abel and Francis Gary Powers stood on opposite sides of the Glienicker Bridge in Berlin. Since World War II, Berlin had been a divided city, with the eastern sector controlled by the Communists and the western sector by a democratic German nation. The Russians had agreed to exchange Powers for Abel and the prisoners were brought to this bridge.

In the mists of a cold February morning, the two men started across the bridge toward each other at the same moment. They passed and returned to their own people without acknowledging each other. Colonel Abel never left his homeland again and Francis Gary Powers gave up his career of making dangerous spy flights. As for Reino Hayhanen, who had decided to make America his home, he had died one night a year earlier in a car accident on the Pennsylvania Turnpike.

Of the three men, Colonel Abel was the highly trained, devoted professional spy. Throughout his trial

and later in an American prison, Abel refused to betray his country or his fellow spies. He had spent years of his life in foreign countries without his family, living in constant danger of capture and even sudden death. To the Russians, Abel was a great hero, and he was rewarded with an important position in the KGB, the Russian intelligence service, in Moscow.

What specific secrets Abel managed to steal from the Americans will probably never be known. But espionage is often a cumulative activity. This means that many small pieces of information are collected by a number of different agents. No one knows which small piece will make an important difference.

Since Colonel Abel was in charge of so many spies and was a high-ranking officer in the KGB, it is conceivable that his contributions were important in giving the Russians inside information about American military production and activities. This in turn may have helped them make decisions about how to handle their own military buildup and what position to take during arms-control negotiations between the Soviet Union and the United States.

Abel's American lawyer, James Donovan, found Abel to be an intelligent man of principle and honor. These heroic traits are to be admired in any man, whether he is a countryman or an enemy agent.

With the production of the U-2 plane, the world entered a new age of espionage in which men and women are sometimes less important than the equipment they use. But even the mechanical spies, the unmanned space satellites, have not totally displaced secret agents.

Who knows, though, what the future holds? Alliances change constantly as countries move closer together in their thinking and in their values. We may look forward to the day in some not-so-distant future when nations will no longer arm themselves, their people will find peaceful means of settling differences, and there will be one united world with no need for international spying or spy heroes.

Bibliography

Boyd, Belle. *Belle Boyd in Camp and Prison*. London: Sauders, Otley, 1865.

Boyle, Andrew. *The Fourth Man*. New York: Dial Press, 1979.

Donovan, James Britt. *Strangers on a Bridge: The Case of Colonel Abel*. New York: Atheneum, 1964.

Dulles, Allen Welsh, ed. *Great True Spy Stories*. New York: Harper and Row, 1968.

Foley, Rae. *Famous American Spies*. New York: Dodd Mead, 1962.

Gainham, Sarah. *The Habsburg Twilight*. New York: Atheneum, 1979.

Graybill, Guy. "The War Which Never Ends." *Espionage Magazine,* Feb. 1986, 26–31.

Hatch, Robert McConnell. *Major John André: A Gallant in Spy's Clothing*. Boston: Houghton Mifflin, 1986.

Hinchley, Vernon. *Spies Who Never Were*. New York: Dodd Mead, 1965.

Horan, James D. *The Pinkertons*. New York: Crown, 1967.

Howe, Russell Warren. *Mata Hari: The True Story*. New York: Dodd Mead, 1986.

Irving, Clifford, and Burkholz, Herbert. *Spy: The Story of Modern Espionage*. New York: Macmillan, 1969.

Kane, Harnett. *Spies for the Blue and Gray*. New York: Doubleday, 1954.

Knightley, Phillip. *The Second Oldest Profession*. New York: W. W. Norton, 1986.

Lamphere, Robert J., and Shactman, Tom. *The FBI-KGB War*. New York: Random House, 1986.

Liddell Hart [Basil Henry Liddell Hart]. *The Man behind the Legend: Colonel Lawrence*. New York: Halcyon House, 1934.

Mack, John E. *A Prince of Our Disorder: The Life of T. E. Lawrence*. Boston: Little, Brown, 1976.

MacLean, Alistair. *Lawrence of Arabia*. New York: Random House, 1962.

Montagu, Ewen. *The Man Who Never Was*. Philadelphia: J. B. Lippincott, 1954.

Nathan, Adele Gutman. *Major John André: Gentleman Spy*. New York: Franklin Watts, 1969.

Page, Bruce; Leitch, David; and Knightley, Phillip. *The Philby Conspiracy*. New York: Doubleday, 1968.

Persico, Joseph E. *Piercing the Reich*. New York: Viking, 1979.

Top Secret: A Dossier of the Greatest Spies of History. Compiled by the editors of *The Reader's Digest*. Pleasantville, N.Y.: Reader's Digest Association, 1974.

Wasserstein, Bernard. *The Secret Lives of Trebitsch Lincoln*. New Haven: Yale University Press, 1988.

Wright, Peter, with Greengrass, Paul. *Spy Catcher*. New York: Viking Penguin, 1987.

Wright, Richard. *Forgotten Ladies*. Philadelphia: J. B. Lippincott, 1928.